A Conversation with Jesus

A Conversation with Jesus

Stephen Seamands

VICTOR BOOKS

A DIVISION OF SCRIPTURE PRESS PUBLICATIONS INC.
USA CANADA ENGLAND

Editors: Carole Streeter, Barbara Williams
Cover Design: Scott Rattray
Cover Photo: Larry Kanfer

Library of Congress Cataloging-in-Publication Data

Seamands, Stephen A., 1949–
    A conversation with Jesus / by Stephen Seamands.
        p.   cm.
    ISBN 1-56476-202-5
    1. Bible. N.T. John XXI, 15-19—Theology.
    2. Bible. N.T. John XX, 19-23—Theology.
    3. Clergy—Office—Biblical teaching. 4. Clergy—
Religious life—Biblical teaching. 5. Clergy—
Appointment, call, and election—Biblical teaching.
I. Title.
BS2615.6.C56S43 1994
226.5'06—dc20   93-43844
                                  CIP

Contents

To my mother
Helen Seamands
whose tenderness, love, and affection
bring joy to my heart

Introduction

You can see it in their hollow eyes. On the surface, everything in their ministry appears to be going well. They are doing all the things ministers are supposed to do—keeping the wheels in the church turning, raising the budget, making sure that what is supposed to happen in the congregation each week does happen. They are not contemplating leaving the ministry—they are still drawing their pay—but they are just going through the motions. The light has gone out inside. You can see it in their empty eyes.

The hopes they once had for congregational renewal have long since been laid aside. They are not expecting anything to happen—except that the ecclesiastical wheels will keep on turning. They are still performing the functions of ministry, but their hearts are no longer in it. They have detached themselves from their congregations.

They entered the ministry with such enthusiasm, but it has not turned out as they thought. Congregational apathy, pettiness, and resistance to change; personal inadequacies and failures; lack of support from denominational leaders— all these along with the constant pressure and stress of the daily grind have worn them down. The passion they once had for ministry has been squeezed out of them. Their expectations, many of them no doubt unrealistic, have been shattered. Disillusionment, the child of false expectation, has set in.

Often coupled with disillusionment is deep-seated anger. They are angry with themselves, the congregation, the denomination. They are angry at God. Everyone they were counting on to help them realize their dreams for ministry has let them down. They feel deceived, betrayed.

They may be unaware of the depth of their anger. By their superficial smiles and disingenuous expressions of concern, they may conceal the anger from their congregations and even themselves, but it is there, seething beneath the surface, eating away at their souls.

Disillusionment and anger breed cynicism. There is an inner sourness about them that makes them scornful of other ministers, especially those who are wholeheartedly engaged in their work. Nothing is more disconcerting to them than the enthusiasm of those who have not lost their passion. When they are with other ministers, their toughness and cynicism often come out. They use humor and sarcasm to ridicule the sincerity of others. They are negative about any proposal to advance God's kingdom. As a result, they are a pain to be with. They are demoralizers. Like a dark cloud, their cynicism weighs heavily upon everyone.

I'm sure you have known such persons, ministers who have lost their passion for ministry. It is a terrible tragedy when it happens, especially when it progresses to the extent that I've just described.

It is easy for it to happen though, because nothing is depleted more quickly in the daily grind than our passion for ministry. One of our constant challenges is to keep it restored and renewed. If we don't, we will be of little use to God or our congregations. Without vision not only do the people perish (Proverbs 29:18), but so also does the ministry.

John Wesley often reminded the early Methodist lay preachers, "You have nothing to do but save souls." Good advice. But I would add that in the process of "saving souls," the most important soul each of us has to save is our own. If in our efforts to save others, we lose our own souls, if we lose our passion for ministry, what good will we be to others?

This book, then, is written to help pastors and those engaged in various forms of Christian ministry to "save their own souls" by restoring their passion for ministry. As I have led retreats and workshops for pastors in various parts of the United States, I have become convinced of the incredible need for such restoration and renewal among ministers. In what follows I have tried to address that need.

One thing is certain: when ministers lose their passion for ministry, they lose perspective. They quickly forget who they are and what ministry is. Spiritual and vocational amnesia sets in. To restore their passion, it is essential for them to be reminded of some basic truths about ministry — truths which they once knew, but have forgotten.

This is exactly what the risen Christ did in His conversation with Peter on the shore of the Sea of Tiberias. When this conversation took place, Peter was a disillusioned, disheartened disciple, if ever there was one. His passion for ministry was gone.

During the Last Supper, he had sworn absolute loyalty to Jesus, "Lord, I am ready to go with You to prison and to death!" (Luke 22:33) only to turn around a few hours later and publicly deny his Lord three times. When he heard the cock crow and realized what he had done, Peter went out and wept bitterly (22:62). Self-assured, self-confident Peter was now a humble, broken man, totally disillusioned with himself.

But Peter was also disillusioned with Jesus. In a moment of revelation, Peter had declared Him to be the promised Messiah, and Jesus had commended him for that. However, Jesus had not turned out to be the Messiah Peter expected. Palm Sunday shouts of "Hosanna! Hosanna!"

soon turned to Good Friday shouts of "Crucify Him! Crucify Him." The One Peter and the others had hoped would redeem Israel (Luke 24:21) was executed in the most degrading manner possible. Some Messiah He turned out to be!

Peter was a totally disillusioned disciple. He was ready to quit. Jesus had called him to fish for people. For three years he had followed Him around learning how to do that, all the while waiting for Jesus to establish the kingdom. Now that idealistic venture was over; it was time to return home and fish for fish again.

Jesus was alive—he knew that. He had appeared several times to Peter and the other disciples. But Peter was still discouraged and confused. After all, you can't base a career on someone who has died and now shows up only occasionally. As for Peter's future as a disciple, there was none. In the light of his out-and-out disloyalty, how could he ever be of any use to Jesus again?

Yet after breakfast on the lakeshore with the disciples, the risen Christ had a conversation with Peter. He didn't shame him. He didn't say, "I told you so. I told you you'd deny Me." Instead Jesus restored Peter as a disciple. He had called him; now He re-called him. He renewed Peter's passion for ministry.

Jesus did this by reminding Peter of the essentials of ministry—truths he already knew but had forgotten. His five words to Peter revolve around key elements in ministry:

- "Do you love Me?"

- "Feed My sheep."
- "You will go where you do not want to go."
- "Follow Me."
- "What is that to you? Follow Me!"

I believe these five words, along with one other — "Receive the Holy Spirit," a word the risen Christ spoke earlier to the disciples in commissioning them to ministry — can also speak to us to restore our passion for ministry. If we will meditate and reflect upon them, they can cause us to remember what ministry truly is. They can restore our sense of calling and rekindle our passion.

In the following chapters, we will consider Jesus' words to us about ministry. I like to think of them as the ordination sermon Jesus preached. Every minister needs to be reminded of these basic elements from time to time. In the hurried practice of ministry, it is so easy to lose sight of who we are and what we are supposed to be doing. When this happens, we soon find ourselves losing our passion.

As we consider them, my prayer is simply that the risen Christ who spoke these words to Peter and the first disciples will speak personally and directly to you. I pray that you will have a conversation with Jesus — a life-changing conversation which will renew your passion for ministry.

Chapter One
Do You Love Me?

*Whatever happens to you, never give up pray-
ing. It would be like giving up breathing. A man
or woman who does not pray is no longer a
minister.*

Henri Nouwen

Do you love Me? . . . Do you love Me? . . . Do you
love Me?" Jesus' first word to Peter is a question,
one He asks him three times. Standing around an
earlier fire in a courtyard, Peter was questioned on three
different occasions about his relationship to Jesus. In each
case he denied that he even knew Him. Now standing near
a fire on the beach, Jesus gives Peter three opportunities to
reaffirm his love and loyalty to Him. He is reinstating Peter
as a disciple. Jesus' threefold question parallel's Peter's
threefold denial.

But Jesus is also seeking to renew Peter's passion for
ministry. Because of his disgraceful failure, Peter has lost his

passion and is ready to quit. He has returned home and gone back to fishing. To renew his passion, Jesus keeps pressing him with this question, "Do you love Me?" because it is the foundational question. All authentic Christian ministry begins and ends with it.

Ministry is like marriage. Why do two persons get married in the first place? Because they love each other and want to spend the rest of their lives sharing their love. And if their marriage is to be successful, it is absolutely essential that they nurture and sustain their love for one another.

Many other things—children, home, work, relatives— emerge out of their love for one another and make demands on their time, energy, and resources. If they are not careful, they can become so consumed with the care and maintenance of the things which come from their love relationship that they neglect the relationship itself.

My wife always knows when this is happening in our marriage. "Steve," she'll say, "when was the last time you told me that you loved me? How long has it been since you and I—just the two of us—spent time together?"

I usually protest, "Carol, you *know* that I love you." Then I recite a long litany of things which ought to prove that I love her. Her response reduces me to silence, "I *know* all that, and I appreciate it. But don't you ever just want to be with me?"

Ministry is somewhat like marriage. How did you get involved in it in the first place? At some point in your life you heard Christ say, "Go." You may have not been sure you heard Him correctly. No doubt your motives for going were mixed. Yet in spite of your ambiguity and uncertainty, you became convinced this was something you had to do. So you went.

But before you heard Christ say, "Go," didn't you first hear Him say, "Come"? "Come to Me, learn of Me, rest in Me, abide in Me." And wasn't your coming the foundation for your going?

"He appointed twelve—designating them apostles—that they might be with Him and that He might send them out to preach" (Mark 3:14). Thus Mark describes the calling of the disciples. They were called to be with Him and to be sent out to preach. The order is significant. First, they were to *be with Him*; then, they were *sent out to preach*.

We observe the same order when Jesus told His disciples, "I am the vine, you are the branches" (John 15:5). Branches exist to bear fruit; if they don't, they are pruned away. But branches can be fruitful only if they abide in the vine. "If a man remains in Me and I in him, he will bear much fruit; apart from Me you can do nothing" (15:5).

Abiding, then, is the primary, fundamental concern of Jesus' disciples. Their foremost calling is to abide in Him. Fruitfulness in ministry is secondary. It is merely a consequence of abiding in Christ.

The Priority of Relationship over Ministry

When we are in ministry, we often lose sight of the priority of abiding. We become so consumed with the work of the church we forget the Lord of the church. Our ministry *for* Christ becomes more important than our relationship *with* Him. Like the church at Ephesus (Revelation 2:1-7), ministers are involved in many good works. But have we too lost our first love, our love for the risen Christ?

Several years ago at a pastor's retreat, I heard Lyle Rader, a retired Salvation Army officer, reminisce about a conversation he had with Samuel Logan Brengle. Brengle was a spiritual giant and an outstanding leader in the Salvation Army during the early decades of this century. Several of his books are still in print today. When Rader was a cadet in officer's training school, Brengle was his friend and mentor.

One day he asked Brengle a question he had wanted to ask for a long time, "Sir, what have been your greatest temptations in ministry?"

Brengle thought for a moment, then he responded, "Actually, I have only *one* temptation in ministry. If I win the battle with this temptation, everything else in my life and ministry falls into place. But if I lose the battle, I soon find myself confronted with all sorts of other temptations."

"What temptation is that?" Rader asked.

"It's the temptation to want to do something *for* God each day, before I've first spent time *with* Him," Brengle replied.

Henri Nouwen received a similar answer to a question he posed to Mother Teresa of Calcutta. Several years ago when he was visiting with her, he asked how he could best fulfill his vocation as a priest. "Spend one hour a day in adoration

of your Lord," she said. "And never do anything you know
is wrong, and you will be all right."

Nouwen was surprised at the simplicity of her response,
but recognized its wisdom. "Like all great disciples of Jesus,
Mother Teresa affirmed again the truth that ministry can be
fruitful only when it grows out of a direct and intimate
encounter with our Lord."[1]

Elizabeth O'Connor of the Church of the Savior in Wash-
ington, D.C. would agree with Mother Teresa. In her book
Call to Commitment she expresses it like this:

> We are not called primarily to create new structures
> for the church in this age; we are not called primari-
> ly to a program of service, or to dream dreams or
> have visions. We are called first of all to belong to
> Jesus Christ as Savior and Lord, and to keep our
> lives warmed at the hearth of His life. It is there the
> fire will be lit which will create new structures and
> programs of service that will draw others into the
> circle to dream dreams and have visions.[2]

Throughout his writings, Oswald Chambers repeatedly
stressed the priority of relationship *with* Christ over ministry *for* Him. Consider the following statements from his
devotional classic, *My Utmost for His Highest:*

> The main thing about Christianity is not the work
> we do, but the relationship we maintain and the

atmosphere produced by that relationship. That is all God asks us to look after, and it is the one thing that is being continually assailed.[3]

We slander God by our very eagerness to work for Him without knowing Him.[4]

The greatest competitor of devotion to Jesus is service for Him.[5]

The great enemy to the Lord Jesus Christ in the present day is the conception of practical work that has not come from the New Testament, but from the systems of the world in which endless energy and activities are insisted upon, but no private life with God.[6]

The central thing about the kingdom of Jesus Christ is a personal relationship to Himself, not public usefulness to men.[7]

We tend to reverse the order, to make the work of ministry primary and relationship with Christ secondary. And so Jesus keeps asking us, as He did Peter, "Do you love Me? . . . Do you love Me? . . . Do you love Me?"

Like Peter, we too are distressed, because He keeps pressing the question. "*Of course* we love You," we insist. "Do You think we would put up with all the hassles of ministry—the stress, the pressure, the criticism, the low salary—if we didn't?"

But Jesus' response reduces us to silence, "Then why do you spend so little time alone in My presence? Don't you ever just want to be with Me?" Or, as one pastor related how Christ put the question to him, "Why, when you're alone with Me, do you only want to 'talk shop'?"

P.T. Forsyth warns ministers not to neglect their own love relationship with Jesus. "It is possible to be so active in the service of Christ as to forget to love Him. Many pastors preach Christ, but get in front of Him by the multiplicity of their own works. It will ruin you if you do."[8] Most of us are aware of the danger of ministry becoming an "activity trap," yet so often we still fall into it. Why?

Why is it so easy to forget to love Christ? Why don't we spend more time alone in His presence—time when we give Him our undivided attention? "When you pray," Jesus said, "go into your room, close the door and pray to your Father, who is unseen" (Matthew 6:6). Why do we have such a hard time doing that? Why are we so quick to rush into the work of ministry, but so slow to nurture our own relationship with Christ? Why don't we love Jesus more?

Too Busy to Pray?

Our immediate response is to point to the incredible time demands of the ministry, and to talk about how busy we are. Be assured, we would like to *pray* more—if we only had time.

Most of us are extremely busy. No question about it. Often we are caught up in such a swirl of activity we are like pinballs in a slot machine. We bounce from one place to another, not knowing where we are going or what we will bump up against next. In the midst of everything, it is extremely difficult to find time to spend alone with Christ.

Furthermore, our congregations exert little pressure on us to cultivate our private life with God. I never had a Pastor-Parish Relations Committee insist that I spend time in prayer, or include prayer in my job description. I also never had a parishioner admonish me for not praying enough.

Churches reward activisim. As we take time to cultivate our relationship with Christ, we will find ourselves moving against the ecclesiastical stream. The demands of ministry will continually encroach upon time set aside for prayer. Unless we set firm boundaries around such scheduled time, it will be stolen away from us.

One pastor schedules "Time with God" in his appointment book. If anyone asks to see him during those times, he says, "Let me check my calendar." He then looks in his book and says, "Sorry, but I already have an appointment then. Could we meet at another time?" Another pastor has instructed her secretary to tell those who ask for her between 8 and 9 A.M., "She can't speak with you now. She's praying. Why don't you call back after 9 o'clock?"

Sometimes we will be misunderstood; we may even seem rigid and uncaring. But we must be strict in guarding time set apart for communion with Christ. As Bishop J.C. Ryle said, "The servants whom the Holy Spirit is to use must resist the tyranny of overwork. They must resolve to be alone with God, even if the hours spent with Him appear to rob others of their service."[9]

We must also learn to commune with God in the midst of our various activities. Thomas Kelly says it well:

> There is a way of ordering our mental life on more than one level at once. On one level we may be thinking, discussing, seeing, calculating, meeting all the demands of external affairs. But deep within, behind the scenes, at a profounder level, we may also be in prayer and adoration, song and worship and a gentle receptiveness to divine breathings.[10]

We must learn to be receptive and active at both levels, especially on those days when, for legitimate reasons, we are unable to spend time alone with God. Regardless of what we are doing—wading through administrative red tape, sitting through committee meetings, preaching a sermon, teaching a Bible study, visiting in the hospital—we can commune with Christ in the midst of our activities, even when we can't commune with Him in solitude.

However, we also need to take a hard honest look at our busyness. Often we complain about how busy we are. We say we don't like it, but actually we do, because it makes us feel significant. It establishes our identity. It proves how much we are needed. What would we do without it?

A seminarian who was serving as an intern in a local church said this to me about her supervisor, the pastor of the church, "He's up at 6 o'clock in the morning and he's on the go until 11 o'clock at night. He never takes a day off. The only time he ever sits down is to eat or to prepare his sermon. But I'm convinced he wouldn't have it any other way. He thrives on being busy."

Sometimes we use our busyness to run from God and ourselves. As long as we are busy, we don't have to face the pain or gnawing emptiness inside. The same seminarian who was concerned about her supervisor's busyness was also concerned about her own. "I still have a lot of pain from my past that I need to work through," she admitted. "But since I've been working here in this church, I've been so busy with other people and their pain that I've neglected my own. When you're helping others, it's easy to pretend you don't need help yourself. But I know that's not healthy. I've got to start taking time for myself again."

Our busyness may also reflect our unbelief. Instead of trusting that God will work through us to accomplish His kingdom purposes, we take upon ourselves the burden of bringing in the kingdom. Ultimately the growth of the kingdom depends on God, not us. "Unless the Lord builds the house, its builders labor in vain" (Psalm 127:1). But from the frantic pace of our ministries you would never know it. Eugene Peterson's words are penetrating, "Busyness is the enemy of spirituality. It is essentially laziness. It is doing the easy thing instead of the hard thing. It is filling our time with our own actions instead of paying attention to God's actions. It is taking charge."[11]

Our busyness reveals what practical atheists we are. By our activism, we act as if God doesn't act! We say we believe in God, but we act as if we could do without Him. That is human arrogance at its worst. It is idolatry. We are worshiping ourselves and our actions instead of God. We need to carefully examine our busyness.

Distorted Concepts of God

There is another reason why ministers find it difficult to cultivate their own relationship with God. Many of us suffer from distorted concepts of God rooted in painful past experiences. These distortions create barriers in our relationship with God. They diminish our desire for fellowship and intimacy with Him.

As ministers we often counsel other people who have distorted concepts of God. In keeping with the God who has been revealed to us in Jesus Christ, we strive to help them develop a mature Christian understanding of God. But what we ourselves believe about God at an intellectual level and what we believe at a feeling level may be quite different. At the feeling level, we may function with the same distorted concepts of God we are seeking to correct in others.

This has become evident to me as I have worked with pastors and Christian leaders in the Doctor of Ministry program at Asbury Seminary. One afternoon in a class, I was leading a group of fifteen in a discussion of the minister's prayer life. We were talking about why we find it difficult to pray. Suddenly a man in the group began to weep for no apparent reason. We waited for him stop. When he finally did, I said to him, "What's the matter? Is there something we can do for you?"

"Not really," he replied. "But as we've been talking, I think I've begun to realize why I find it so difficult to pray.

"About five years ago my wife left me. That came as a great shock to me—I never thought it could happen to me. Yet I was still sure that God wouldn't let our separation end in divorce. Somehow He would bring us back together. After all, isn't divorce against His will? And hadn't He called me into the ministry? What would divorce do to that? So I prayed and I prayed, because I was sure God was going to come through.

"But He didn't. My marriage ended in divorce. And now I'm afraid to really trust God with anything significant in my life. I'm afraid that if I do, He will let me down again. It hurt so much the last time. I've been burned once; I don't want to be burned again."

All of us understood why this minister found it difficult to pray. If you have ever felt abandoned, forsaken, or betrayed by God, it is extremely difficult to trust Him. In fact, it makes you angry at God. You were counting on Him, but He didn't come through. That hurts. And when you feel hurt by God, it is natural to want to lash out against Him.

You will find it extremely difficult to spend time in His presence. You will find yourself avoiding Him—just as you would avoid anyone who has hurt you by letting you down.

A year later as I was teaching that class and we were discussing the same subject—why ministers have difficulty with prayer—a similar thing happened. "As we've been sitting here talking," one of the pastors said, "I think I'm beginning to understand why I find it difficult to pray.

"My father was an extremely competitive man. He was always pushing my brothers and me to excel, especially in athletics. When I was in high school, I was on the basketball team. One night I played the game of my life. I was so proud of myself. I had scored twenty-nine points—my all-time high. And I was so much looking forward to going home and talking about the game with Dad. I knew he would be very proud of me. I couldn't wait to hear him brag on me and tell me how well I had played.

"I got home, and Dad did say, 'You played a good game, Son.' But then he proceeded to tell me five or six things I should have done to have played better. When he did that my heart sank. I was so hurt and disappointed. I thought I had done my best, but it still wasn't good enough for him.

"I've heard it said that our feelings about our earthly father affect our understanding of our Heavenly Father. If that's true, then I think I understand why it's hard for me to spend time alone with God. I'm afraid God is going to treat me the same way my father did that day. He's going to say, 'Yes, you are a good pastor. You're doing quite well. But if

you'd only do this and this and this, you'd be much better.'
I already feel I'm doing my best; I don't want to hear that.''

Again everyone in the class understood exactly what he
was saying. Nobody wants to spend time with someone who
can never be satisfied, someone who is always demanding
that you do more. We avoid people like that.

These and other experiences with ministers have convinced me that although our theology may be correct, and
we may be experts in helping others work through their
misconceptions of God, at the feeling level we often oper-
ate with misconceptions too—misconceptions which diminish our desire to spend time in God's presence. No one
wants to spend time with an ogre! If we conceive of God
that way, we will find it extremely difficult to pray. In fact,
we probably won't.

We need to search our hearts to see if there is any mis-
conception of God, rooted in past painful experiences,
which is undermining our prayer life. We may be angry with
God. We may have felt terribly let down by Him at some
point in our lives. We may be afraid to come into His presence because of what we think He is going to demand of us.
Before we experience a renewed prayer life, one where we
delight to come into God's presence, we may first need to
find healing for some hurt in the past.

Praying according to the Flesh

We also encounter difficulty in prayer when we take the
burden of prayer upon ourselves, when we assume that

prayer is something *we* have to do, rather than something *God* through the Holy Spirit does in us. Prayer then becomes a work of the flesh, an activity based upon self-effort and striving rather than a work of the Spirit.[12] Whenever this happens, failure and frustration are inevitable.

Paul admonished the Galatian Christians because they had made this very mistake, not only in relation to prayer but also in relation to the Christian life as a whole. "Are you so foolish?" he asked them. "After beginning with the Spirit, are you now trying to attain your goal by human effort?" (Galatians 3:3) They had received salvation as a gift from God through faith in Christ; now they were trying to work out their salvation by their own self-effort. They had been initiated into life in Christ through the Spirit; now they were trying to live that life in the power of the flesh.

Paul then spelled out the problem for them: "For the sinful nature [flesh] desires what is contrary to the Spirit, and the Spirit what is contrary to the sinful nature" (5:17). How could they walk according to the Spirit in the power of the flesh? The two are antithetical. The Spirit working in us causes us to love God and obey His commandments, but "the sinful mind [flesh] is hostile to God. It does not submit to God's law, nor can it do so. Those controlled by the sinful nature cannot please God" (Romans 8:7-8).

When prayer becomes a work of the flesh, it is no wonder that we experience frustration and failure. We are asking something which is opposed and hostile to God to draw near to Him and enjoy being in His presence. It is like asking darkness to have fellowship with light!

Of course, the "the flesh" can say prayers—eloquent ones at that. There is a religion of the flesh, a religion which attempts to keep the commandments through human effort. Outwardly it can be quite impressive. As a former Pharisee, Paul knew that more than anyone else. But prayer as intimate communion and fellowship with God? The flesh can never effect that. Only the Holy Spirit can. So Paul urged the Galatians, "Live by the Spirit, and you will not gratify the desires of the sinful nature" (Galatians 5:16).

We will never overcome our prayerlessness by self-effort. We must learn to "pray in the Holy Spirit" (Jude 20). Andrew Murray was right, "Prayer is just the breathing of the Spirit in us; power in prayer comes from the power of the Spirit in us, waited on and trusted in."[13]

When we begin to pray, then we should acknowledge our inability to pray and our total dependency upon the Holy Spirit (see Romans 8:26-27). We should invite the Holy Spirit to come and pray in us and through us. By faith, we should receive the Spirit who enables us to pray, knowing that our Father in heaven will "give the Holy Spirit to those who ask Him!" (Luke 11:13)

The words of Isaac Watts' wonderful hymn, "Come, Holy Spirit, Heavenly Dove," should be on our lips. In the first verse he calls upon the Holy Spirit:

Come, Holy Spirit, heavenly Dove,
With all Thy quickening powers;

Kindle a flame of sacred love
In these cold hearts of ours.

The next two verses poignantly describe our predicament in prayer and devotion when we are left to ourselves:

Look how we grovel here below,
Fond of these earthly toys;
Our souls, how heavily they go,
To reach eternal joys.

In vain we tune our formal songs,
In vain we strive to rise;
Hosannas languish on our tongues,
And our devotion dies.

And so we wonder, is this all we can hope for? Is our predicament permanent?

And shall we then forever live
At this poor dying rate?
Our love so faint, so cold to Thee,
And Thine to us so great!

No. There is a better way. There is a divine enabling through the Holy Spirit. In the final verse, Watts invokes the Spirit again:

Come, Holy Spirit, heavenly Dove,
With all Thy quickening powers;
Come, shed abroad a Savior's love,
And that shall kindle ours.[14]

We must learn to pray *for* the Spirit and *in* the Spirit. Otherwise prayer will be a continual exercise in frustration.

Fear of Losing Ourselves

There is an even deeper reason why we find it difficult to pray. We instinctively know that in the presence of God we will have to face our true selves. We are afraid that if we get too close to God we will lose ourselves in the process. Henri Nouwen's book *The Way of the Heart* helped me to understand our elemental fear of prayer as I never had before. It is a study of the spirituality of the Desert Fathers of the ancient church and its relevance for contemporary ministry.

The Desert Fathers understood prayer and solitude, time spent alone in the presence of God, as a "furnace of transformation." At the very beginning of His ministry, Christ Himself passed through this furnace when the Spirit drove Him into the wilderness to be tempted (Matthew 4:1-11). All of His temptations—to turn stones into bread, to jump down from the temple, to worship the devil—were Satan's attempts to get Him to wrongly assert Himself, to find His identity in Himself rather than in His Father. But in each case Jesus overcame the temptation by dying to Himself and entrusting Himself and His ministry totally to God. For Jesus the furnace of prayer and solitude involved both a great struggle and a great encounter. The same holds true for us. In the struggle, we die to the compulsions of the false self; in the encounter, we meet Christ and discover our true self in Him.

But how do the great struggle and the great encounter work out in the actual practice of prayer? Nouwen explains:

> In solitude I get rid of my scaffolding: no friends to talk with, no telephone calls to make, no meetings to attend, no music to entertain, no books to distract, just me—naked, vulnerable, weak, sinful, deprived, broken, nothing. It is this nothingness that I have to face in my solitude, a nothingness so dreadful that everything in me wants to run to my friends, my work, and my distractions so that I can forget my nothingness and make myself believe that I am worth something. But that is not all. As soon as I decide to stay in my solitude, confusing ideas, disturbing images, wild fantasies, and weird associations jump about in my mind like monkeys in a banana tree. Anger and greed begin to show their ugly faces. I give long hostile speeches to my enemies and dream lustful dreams in which I am wealthy, influential, and very attractive. . . . Thus I try again to run from the dark abyss of my nothingness and restore my false self in all its vainglory.[15]

This, then, is the struggle of solitude: to die to the false self and to persevere until all the disturbing internal voices have quieted down. But this struggle is far beyond our own strength. As the Desert Fathers recognized, "Anyone who wants to fight his demons with his own weapons is a fool."[16]

Thus, out of the struggle of solitude and prayer emerges the great encounter where we embrace Christ and totally surrender ourselves to Him. Only as we cling to Him and rest in His love are we able to survive the struggle of our solitude. Only in the presence of His grace are we able to face our sin. In solitude, then, we focus our attention, not upon the many voices that assail us, but upon the living Christ. As Nouwen puts it:

> Only with a single-minded attention to Christ can we give up our clinging fears and face our own true nature. As we come to realize that it is not we who live, but Christ who lives in us, that He is our true self, we can slowly let our compulsions melt away and begin to experience the freedom of the children of God.[17]

Why, then, do we run from prayer and solitude and rush into ministry? The Desert Fathers discerned the central issue: We are afraid of our nothingness, so we cling to the compulsions of our false self. We instinctively know that if we spend too much time in the presence of Jesus, we will have to come to terms with those compulsions, and that will be painful, fearful, risky. It will mean letting go, dying to the things we've been holding onto for security.

What we are so afraid of is actually our salvation. In the furnace of transformation, we encounter Jesus Himself. "It is I," He assures us. "Be not afraid." When we are crucified with Christ, we don't die, as we are prone to think; rather, we begin to truly live. We live because He lives within us (Galatians 2:20). When the old self dies, the new self—our true self—lives; and then, set free from the tyranny of the old self, we begin to experience the glorious liberty of being God's children.

A Challenge and an Invitation

"Do you love Me?... Do you love Me?... Do you love Me?" This is the foundational question. Jesus keeps pressing Peter with it, and He presses us with it too. It is a question which calls us to cultivate our relationship with Christ by spending time alone in His presence. But as we have explored some of the reasons why we find it difficult to do this, you may have become disheartened. Our discussion may have made you more aware of how much you have failed in nurturing your own relationship with Christ. "No, I don't love Jesus very much," you may say. "I don't spend enough time in His presence." In case you are feeling that way, let me conclude this chapter by reminding you of two things.

First, the question to Peter is a challenge, but it's also an invitation. Remember, Jesus asks the question not to condemn Peter, but to reinstate him as a disciple. The threefold question parallels his threefold denial. Like Peter, you and I fail over and over again in our efforts to be faithful disciples. But the fact that you are feeling the force of the question indicates that you are being reinstated as well. You have failed to love Jesus as you should, but in pressing you with the question, "Do you love Me?" He is inviting you back, calling you to a deeper level of intimacy with Himself.

Second, Jesus will accept you where you are, if you are simply honest with Him. There has been much discussion about the two different Greek words for love which are used in the dialogue between Jesus and Peter. The first two times Jesus asks Peter, "Do you *love* Me?" the Greek verb *agapeo* is used. Throughout the New Testament *agapeo* denotes the highest form of love—sacrificial, Godlike love. But the first two times when Peter answers, "You know that I *love* You," he uses the Greek verb *phileo*. Signifying brotherly or sisterly love, *phileo* is not as high a form of love as *agapeo*.

However, the third time Jesus asks Peter the question, He does not use *agapeo* but *phileo*. And once again, Peter answers with the same verb. Biblical commentators debate whether there is significance in this. Are the two words synonymous throughout, or are we to find some meaning in the difference? Although we shouldn't read too much into it, I find it significant that in using *phileo* the third time, rather than *agapeo*, Jesus comes down to Peter's level. He is saying to Peter, "You've denied Me three times, and so there's no way you can say you love Me with the kind of sacrificial, self-giving love that I have for you. But that's all right, Peter. I accept you where you are. You're sure about your brotherly love for Me, so let's start with that. Together, we'll move on from there."

Jesus relates to us in the same way. He comes down to our level and starts with us where we are. Regardless of how inadequate we believe our love for Jesus is, we can take heart. He hasn't given up on us. He is ready to begin with us again.

But we need to be honest with Him about where we are. The third time Jesus asked, "Do you love Me?" Peter was hurt that He had asked the question again. So Peter said to Jesus, "Lord, You know all things; You know that I love You" (John 21:17). Peter was saying, "Lord, You know exactly where I am." He was perfectly honest with Jesus about his condition. When you and I are honest, Jesus can help us too. Yet sometimes that is so hard for us as ministers. We are always in a position of helping others, but we find it hard to admit that we need help.

Be ruthlessly honest with Jesus. Like Peter, acknowledge, "Lord, You know everything. You know exactly where I am. You know about my lack of love for You. Help me to love You more. Put within me a desire to spend time in Your presence. Show me why I have a hard time doing that."

When you are honest about your lack of love for Jesus, He can do something with that!

Chapter Two
Feed My Sheep

*Feed My sheep — identify yourself with My inter-
ests in other people, not identify Me with your
interests in other people.*

Oswald Chambers

ach time, the risen Christ's question to Peter,
"Do you love Me?" is followed by a command,
"Feed My lambs.... Take care of My sheep.
... Feed My sheep." These words must have been tremendously reassuring to Peter. After his great personal failure, he has lost all confidence in himself. He
doubts if he'll ever be fit for ministry again. By com-
manding Peter to feed His sheep, Jesus is saying,
"Peter, I know what you've done and how you feel,
but I still believe in you. There's no question in My
mind about your suitability for ministry. You are the
rock upon which I am going to build My church. You

are to shepherd My people. Go now and feed My sheep."

Through this command, then, Jesus is reassuring Peter. He is reinstating him as a disciple, declaring him fit for ministry. But through this command, Jesus is also reminding Peter of his essential calling as a minister. He is to be a shepherd who feeds and tends Christ's sheep. Above all others, this image defines what ministers are and what they do. "Feed My sheep" is Christ's principal command to Peter and also to us.

The fact that it is a command is significant. We are to feed the sheep both in and out of season, when we feel like it and when we don't. This may seem to contradict what was said in the last chapter about ministry flowing out of love for Christ. Now we simply have a command, "Just do it, whether you are inspired by love or not." How do the two fit together?

We are to feed the sheep both *because we love Christ* and *because He has commanded us to do it*. Each leads us to the other. Love for Christ leads to obedience, and obedience to His command leads to love. Often we don't feel the force of both. We may feed the sheep purely out of a sense of duty. We may say, "Even though it's the last thing on earth I want to do, I'm still going to do it." But in simply doing it out of a sense of duty, we place ourselves in a position where love can ignite.

When I was a pastor, I would sometimes drive to a hospital late in the afternoon to visit a parishioner. Often I had been busy all day and was worn out. I was ready to go home, to relax and eat, and spend time with my family before returning to the church for a meeting in the evening. The last person I wanted to see was a patient in the hospital.

While riding the elevator up to the person's room, I would pray, "Lord, You know I don't really want to be here. You know how tired I am. But I give myself to You. Take me and use me as I visit with this person."

Then I entered the room and began visiting, and before long, my parishioner was sharing his or her deepest concerns with me and I was engaged in a significant time of ministry. Like the two men walking on the road to Emmaus (Luke 24:13-35), we knew that the risen Christ was in our midst. When I finally left the room, I was on cloud nine. My passion for ministry had been renewed. Most of all, I was thanking Christ for the privilege of being a co-laborer with Him. How different the elevator ride down was from the ride up!

"Feed My sheep." Sometimes we feed them because the love of Christ inspires us; at other times, it is simply because we have been commanded to. Sometimes delight leads to duty; at other times duty leads to delight. The two are not opposed to each other, because one leads to the other.

The Words of the Command

Each word in the command is significant. The first is actually two different Greek words: "feed" is from *boskein,* and "tend" is from *poimainen.* Feeding has to do with supplying food and nourishment for the flock. Tending carries with it the idea of ruling over and governing.

As part of a command, these words force us to examine ourselves. Are we doing these things? Shepherds may do many things, but neglect what is most important: feeding and tending the sheep. The Prophet Ezekiel rebuked the shepherds of Israel for this very reason:

> This is what the Sovereign Lord says: Woe to the shepherds of Israel who only take care of themselves! Should not shepherds take care of the flock? You eat the curds, clothe yourselves with the wool and slaughter the choice animals, but you do not take care of the flock (Ezekiel 34:2-3).

We need to ask ourselves, "Are we feeding the sheep or feeding ourselves?" We may be filling up our schedules with many worthwhile activities, but are we doing what we've been called to do? What Christ has commanded us to do? Shepherds are supposed to feed sheep!

Are we paying the price necessary to prepare good food? The wife of a college classmate of mine was talking about meals in their home. "There's a big difference between 'preparing meals' and 'getting food,' " she said. "Preparing meals takes time and effort. But getting food—you can do that on the run. You pick up something at a fast-food restaurant on the way home from work. Or just grab something out of the freezer, pop it in the microwave, and presto, you've got food. Because of our busy schedules, at our house we do very little of the first—preparing meals—and a lot of the second—getting food."

I thought about what she said in relation to the way ministers prepare sermons. You can get prepackaged food for the flock by subscribing to a sermon service. You can hastily throw together a "Saturday night special," or you can prepare a meal by spending time in prayer, meditating upon a text, studying it, wrestling with it, and then crafting a sermon from it. To do so takes time and energy and persistence. Gardner Taylor reminds us that sermon preparation is sweet torture. Preparing good food for the flock is costly for the shepherd.

Are we providing the flock with a healthy and balanced diet? We may be giving our congregations plenty of appetizers and desserts—what they seem to enjoy most—but are we neglecting the less palatable but more nutritious meats and vegetables they also need?

By the diet we provide, are we keeping the congregation in a state of spiritual infancy? The New Testament often contrasts mature and immature Christians, those who only drink liquids like milk and those who consume solid food

(1 Corinthians 3:1-2; Ephesians 4:13-15; Hebrews 5:12-14; 1 Peter 2:2). Because so many are spiritually immature, it is tempting to avoid teaching or preaching anything that is difficult, that will stretch our parishioners' minds or run counter to their prejudices. "My congregation would never understand that," we think to ourselves. "It would bore them to death." So we never really confront the problem of spiritual immaturity or help people grow to spiritual adulthood.

"Feed. . . . Tend" The first word in the commands makes us examine ourselves. Are we doing what shepherds are supposed to do? Are we doing it well?

The second word in the command is the pronoun "My." It reminds us of something we often forget, that the sheep are not ours; they belong to Christ. We are stewards, not owners. Realizing this ought to affect the way we treat those entrusted to our care.

When I borrow a tool from my neighbor, I am generally much more careful with it than when I am using one of my own. If one of my sons picks up my neighbor's tool, I am quick to caution him to be careful with it. Why? Because the tool is not mine. It belongs to someone else. I want to return it to my neighbor in the same condition as when I borrowed it.

"Feed *My* lambs. . . . Tend *My* sheep." They are not mine, they are His, and I need to treat them accordingly. As Charles Jefferson suggests, this "My" is "the mightiest pronoun in the New Testament for the saving of the minister from lordliness.''[1] Christ is the Chief Shepherd; we are only His undershepherds. The sheep belong to Him. We must minister to them in a manner pleasing to Him.

The "My" also brings us back to the question, "Do you love Me?" For how will we ever know what He wants for His sheep if we don't stay in close contact with Him? Occasionally when one of our children has been staying overnight with a friend, I have received a telephone call from the parents of the friend asking permission to take our child somewhere. "The kids want us to take them to a movie," they may say. "But since that wasn't a part of the plan when your child came over, we thought we ought to call and ask if it would be all right with you to do that."

"Sure," I will say. "Go right ahead. But thanks for calling and asking. I appreciate your consideration."

Why did they feel obligated to call? Because they are not my child's parents and have not been given authority over my child. So they didn't feel right about taking my child somewhere without first getting permission from me.

The sheep we are called to shepherd belong to Christ. We've got to stay in close communication with Him in order to know what He wants for His sheep.

The third words in the command are "lambs" from *arnion* and "sheep" from *probaton*. The shepherd is to feed and tend both kinds of sheep—the young lambs who are innocent and weak, and the adult sheep who are stronger but more stubborn. This is not easy. No class of livestock requires more careful handling and detailed direction than sheep.

Sheep are timid and fearful. They are so easily panicked that even a stray jackrabbit suddenly bounding out of a bush can stampede a whole flock. When one startled sheep starts running, a dozen others will follow it in blind fear, even though they have no idea what frightened them. Sheep are helpless, feeble creatures with almost no means of self-defense. In the face of danger their only recourse is to run.

But sheep are also stiff-necked and stubborn. They follow their own fancies and insist on their own ways (Isaiah 53:6). As a result they often get themselves into the most preposterous situations, from which they cannot escape. In *A Shepherd Looks at Psalm 23*, Philip Keller tells how his sheep, greedy for another mouthful of green grass, would climb down steep cliffs where they then slipped and fell into the sea. One winter day he spent several hours rescuing a ewe who kept doing this over and over. Her stubbornness was her undoing.[2] Parishioners, like lambs and sheep, are not easy to look after. At times they can drive a pastor crazy. They require wise and patient care. Some are timid and fearful; others are stubborn and headstrong. Christ has commanded us to feed and tend them all.

The Motives of a Minister

As ministers, what should motivate us to obey Christ's command? Jesus doesn't explicitly address the issue of motivation in His conversation with Peter, although it is implicit in the question, "Do you love Me?" But it is an important issue to consider, since we may be feeding the sheep but doing it for the wrong reasons. What ought to be our motives for ministry?

In his first epistle, Peter himself addresses this question. Christ's command, "Feed My Sheep," must have been deeply impressed upon his mind, for years later he uses the same image when he writes to the elders in the churches. "Be shepherds of God's flock that is under your care," he says. Then he speaks to the issue of motivation. "Serving as overseers—not because you must, but because you are willing, as God wants you to be; not greedy for money, but eager to serve; not lording it over those entrusted to you, but being examples to the flock" (1 Peter 5:1-3). Here Peter mentions three improper motivations for ministry. Let's consider them one at a time.

1. Not because you must, but because you are willing. Ministry can flow out of an unhealthy inner drivenness. Ministers may be workaholics, perfectionists, or codependents. Some have an inordinate desire to please others. There are those who seek everyone's approval, those who must prove to themselves they can succeed, those who need to be needed, even those who use the ministry to atone for their own sins.

"When a Healer Needs Healing," the cover story of a recent issue of *Parade*, revealed that many who are struggling in the ministry today are driven by a compulsiveness rooted in unresolved childhood problems. Paul Rasmus, an Episcopal priest, describes his experience:

I came from a dysfunctional home and had zero self-esteem. . . . I find that a lot of us, growing up, wanted to save our families—but, when that was impossible, we went out to save the world. We're generally workaholics, and we're great at fixing other people, but we don't have the foggiest notion of what to do for ourselves.[3]

Dr. Wayne Fehr, director of spiritual care at Saint Barnabas Center, an ecumenical treatment center for clergy in Oconomowoc, Wisconsin, agrees.

A substantial number come from that background, and they share an excessive, compulsive absorption in work, to the neglect of their personal needs. There's a deeply rooted, overwhelming need to please others, to take care of everybody else, to avoid conflict—but at some point it becomes too hard, and everything breaks down.[4]

"Not compulsively, but willingly." Peter's warning is more timely than ever. Does our feeding of the sheep flow out of a diseased emotional system? Or does it flow out of emotional health?

2. Not greedy for money, but eager to serve. Some ministers use congregations not to gratify emotional hungers, but for material gain or career enhancement. A district superintendent expressed his deep concern several years ago over

some pastors in his care who were in the ministry primarily for the benefits—the job security, pension, guaranteed appointment, and minimum salary.

"The ministry is really not that bad a deal," he said. "Once you're ordained, the system takes care of you. Unless you really blow it, you're not going to to get fired. What's more, you don't really have to work that hard to make it in the ministry. In fact, you can do very little and still get by."

For some the sordid gain is not the security and benefits of the ministry. It is using a congregation as a stepping-stone for career advancement. "I'll work hard in this church, and the congregation will grow," the minister reasons. "Then I'll be respected by my colleagues. I'll be sought after by other churches in the denomination, and my superiors will reward me with a larger and more prominent church." So the minister simply uses the present congregation to get to the next one. He or she becomes like a strip miner who plunders the resources of the land and then moves on.

A minister from Texas observed, "Too many of us make our career decisions on the basis of the Four Ps—the size of the Paycheck, the condition of the Parsonage, the prominence of the Pulpit, and the security of the Pension." All, of course, are legitimate concerns, but when they become ultimate—and it's so easy for that to happen—we are ministering for sordid gain.

3. Not lording it over those entrusted to you, but being examples to the flock. Some persons are in ministry be-

cause of their passion for power, their craving for control, their longing for the limelight. The staff members in a certain church nicknamed the senior pastor King Arthur. "He has to have his hands on everything that happens around here," the custodian complained to me. "I can hardly put a new roll of toilet paper in the bathroom without getting his permission."

Pastors often lament the lack of lay involvement in their churches. "This congregation expects me to do everything," they complain. "Don't they know anything about the priesthood of all believers?" But pastors themselves are often the greatest obstacle to increased lay ministry. They are afraid to let go of the reins, to give up control, to allow things to be done any other way but theirs. The truth is that they enjoy doing everything themselves.

"Feed My sheep." That is Christ's command. But what is motivating us do it? Are we doing it willingly, eagerly, as an example to the flock? Peter reminds the elders, "When the Chief Shepherd appears, you will receive the crown of glory that will never fade away" (1 Peter 5:4). Are we serving them because of our love for Christ, the Chief Shepherd? Are we looking for His approval or someone else's? Are we seeking a temporal, fading reward or an eternal one? What are our motives for ministry?

Refining Our Motives for Ministry

Of course, God doesn't wait until our motives are 100 percent pure before calling us to ministry. If He did, no one would be in ministry! All of us enter ministry with mixed motives—many of which are subconscious. But although God accepts us as we are, He doesn't leave us where we are. God works to purify and refine our motives, often using our ministry setting as a crucible for the refining process. While God is working *through* us as we minister in a particular setting, He uses that same setting to work *on* us to purge our impure motives.

I have found this to be true throughout my ministry. I'll never forget my first pastorate. What a mess the church was in when I arrived! After I had been there a few months, we had a cleanup day at the church. Our motto was, "When in doubt, out!" We hauled away three truckloads of junk from the church that day. Some of the old Sunday School material must have been thirty-five years old! The rundown physical appearance of the church, the messiness and the clutter, reflected the state of the church in almost every other area as well.

But in some ways, inheriting such a desperate situation was to my advantage. After all, the only way we could go was up. And we did go up. The first year and a half of my ministry there was wonderful. Worship attendance climbed. A successful fund-raising campaign enabled us to make major repairs on the church plant. The congregation began to come alive spiritually. We had a dynamic lay witness mission. Bible studies and other small groups were launched. A men's prayer breakfast led to a ministry in a local prison. A Mother's Morning Out met spiritual and social needs of those with preschool children. There was excitement and expectancy in our worship services. God was present in our midst.

During that period of time I was riding high. It's fun to be a pastor when people think you're a messiah! But then our progress leveled off. Attendance plateaued. There were no big events to look forward to, no major initiatives to be launched—just the weekly routine of church life. From my perspective, very little seemed to be happening.

As a result, I found myself concerned and anxious, sometimes even depressed. The church was no longer moving ahead according to my timetable. I had grandiose visions of turning the church into another Crystal Cathedral, but it was becoming crystal clear that wasn't going to happen.

The congregation was so happy with the way things were. From their perspective, the church was so much better than before. They wanted to sit back and enjoy it for a while. But I wasn't satisfied, and I was angry at them for their complacency. I found myself thinking, "You don't deserve to have someone as gifted as I am for your pastor. Maybe I should ask the district superintendent for a new appointment."

Then God began to use my anger, frustration, and discouragement as a crucible to refine one of my impure motives for ministry. As the heat was turned up, I began to realize what I was doing. Yes, I was feeding the sheep, but I was feeding them in order to feed myself. I was using the ministry to get my own ego needs met, especially my need for significance. I was basing my significance as a person on

achieving success in ministry. As long as we were progressing according to my schedule and my definition of success,
I was happy. But now that the church wasn't progressing in
that fashion, I felt like a failure.

One day as I was praying, God asked me a penetrating
question. "Steve, what are you really in the ministry for? Are
you in the ministry to build My kingdom, or are you in it to
build yours?" I didn't like God's question because I knew
the answer. But since I couldn't evade the issue, I began to
wrestle with it as never before.

Early one Sunday morning several months later, my wrestling came to a head. I was alone in the sanctuary, standing
behind the pulpit practicing my sermon, preaching it as if
the congregation were there. My sermon was based upon
the story of Abraham and the sacrifice of his son, Isaac. I
wanted the congregation to realize that like Abraham, all of
us have "Isaacs" in our lives. Although they are God's pre-
cious gifts to us, we often make idols out of them, worshiping the gifts instead of the Giver. So God has to bring us to
the place where we're willing to give them up and worship
Him alone.

While I was practicing, a strange thing happened—I ap-
plied my sermon to myself! My Isaac was the ministry God
had given me. I had made an idol out of it and was using it
to establish my self-worth instead of simply receiving it as a
gift from God.

Before I knew it, my eyes were filled with tears. I stopped
practicing my sermon in mid-sentence, put my head down

on the pulpit and began to pray, "Lord, take it—take my ministry," I cried. "And if You want me to spend the rest of my life in this church, and if it never gets any bigger than it is now, I'll do it, if that's what You want. Take me, I'm Yours."

As I reflect now on that prayer, I wonder how much I really meant it. But I believe I meant it enough so that God was able to answer it. God was able to purge an improper motivation for ministry. He began a process of refining so that more and more I was ministering to build His kingdom, not mine.

The next three and a half years in that church were the best ones I spent there. Not because the church became what I had envisioned—it never did—but because my ministry had been liberated from the success syndrome. I was free now to simply love the people and lead them at a pace right for them. I was no longer feeding them in order to feed myself.

Then I moved to another church, and it wasn't long before the refining process began again. How different my new congregation was from my former one. I followed a pastor who had stayed there only two years. He had had a very difficult time because the congregation was grieving over the loss of his predecessor, a pastor who had served the church for seventeen years.

Now I was there, and as I began to lead, I was moving the congregation in new directions. But a core of longtime members frowned on that. During their former pastor's long tenure, the church had become stagnant and set in its ways. Now they resisted the changes that were taking place. Most of all, they felt threatened by the growing number of newcomers in the church.

As a result, I found myself in a crossfire of criticism. The people in my former church were so gracious and kind. They knew I was insecure and needed affirmation, so they gave it to me. But not these folks! They were harsh and critical. They were downright mean, and it hurt.

Once again I was in a crucible — one which God used to refine another impure motivation for ministry. Out of that crucible of criticism, I began to realize how desperately I needed acceptance and approval, and how much I needed to be liked by everybody. I came to see what an "approvalholic" I was.

I also came to see how impossible it is to truly minister to people when you must have their approval. If you are going to act in their best interests, you often have to do and say things which initially will be painful to them. But if you're always walking on eggshells around them because you're overly concerned about how they will react, you'll never do or say the difficult thing for fear of being rejected.

One day, in the heat of that crucible, God asked another penetrating question, "Steve, you know I love you and approve of you." "Yes, Lord," I responded. "Of course, I do. And I know Your love and acceptance are unconditional." Then came the question, "Isn't My love and approval enough? Do you have to have everyone else's too?" Ouch!

Suddenly I realized what I had been doing. I saw myself as Adam in the Garden. God was saying, "Eat the fruit of all these trees in the Garden. You have My blessing and approval." But my response was, "That's not enough. I've got to have everyone else's approval too."

In that moment, I saw the utter sinfulness of what I had been doing. "O, God," I cried, "I repent of my sin. Forgive me for what I've done. Cleanse my heart and set me free."

God heard my prayer and began to purge another impure motivation for ministry. I was ministering in order to get other people's approval. God began to refine and purify in order to get me to the place where His approval truly was enough. I no longer needed everyone else's. I was free now to speak the truth in love. I could even give others permission not to like me!

God continues to purify and refine my motives for ministry. There are other crucible experiences I could describe, but those I have given are sufficient to exhibit a common pattern in many of our lives. While God works through us, He also works on us, refining our impure motives for ministry so that we can become vessels more fit for His use.

"Feed My lambs. Tend My sheep." Examine your ministry in the light of Christ's command. You may be doing many seemingly good things, but are you feeding the sheep?

And why are you feeding them? Are you feeding them in order to feed yourself? What are the motives in your ministry which need purging? Will you offer them to Jesus, the great refiner? He will cleanse and purify them if you do.

Chapter Three
Where You Do Not Want to Go

The work of God can be built only upon the ruins of ourselves.

Fenelon

I n April 1978 I awoke one morning with a pain in my stomach. By noon it had shifted over to my right side. By 4 o'clock that afternoon, I was in the hospital with what a surgeon called "a textbook case of appendicitis." The surgery was routine and uneventful, and I went home several days later.

But I will always remember that experience, since it was the first time in my adult life I had been a patient in a hospital. I was given a gown to wear which didn't quite cover me. I was left sitting in a wheelchair in a cold, drafty hallway for what seemed like an eternity while I waited to get an X-ray. I was lifted off my bed by several orderlies and a nurse, placed on a litter, and transported to the operating room. While I was recovering, I was talked to and treated as if I were a helpless child.

All these things combined to produce within me a sense of powerlessness, of losing control of my own destiny. I was no longer an independent adult, in charge of my life. I was a dependent child, and others were setting my course for me. It was a disconcerting blow to my pride and self-confidence.

But I was also thankful for the experience, because it made me a better pastor. From that point on when I visited people in the hospital, I had more empathy for them. Now I understood firsthand what they were going through.

I am reminded of that experience by Jesus' third word to Peter. The first word was a question, "Do you love Me?" The second was a command, "Feed My sheep." The third is a prediction, "I tell you the truth, when you were younger you dressed yourself and went where you wanted; but when you are old you will stretch out your hands, and someone else will dress you and lead you where you do not want to go" (John 21:18).

Jesus is painting a picture of a feeble old man who can't dress himself anymore. He is incontinent. His vision is blurred. He totters when he walks. He is no longer in control of his destiny. He is at the mercy of others as to what he does and where he goes. And Jesus is saying, "Peter, one day you are going to be like that."

Following this prediction, John explains what Jesus

meant, "Jesus said this to indicate the kind of death by which Peter would glorify God" (21:19). Jesus is predicting that just as He did, Peter too will die an unnatural death. And that, of course, is what happened. According to tradition and modern scholarship, Peter was martyred in Rome during the time of intense persecution under Nero.

An inspiring, though not necessarily reliable, story of how that occurred soon spread among Christians and was later narrated by church fathers such as Origen and Ambrose.[1] According to the story, when persecution broke out, Peter was seized by the Roman authorities and thrown into prison. Because his leadership was so crucial to the church, the other Christian leaders in Rome insisted he should attempt to escape and flee the city. But Peter was reluctant. He didn't want to be accused of cowardice in the face of death. He also wanted to encourage others who were suffering for their faith. Only after much pleading was he willing to go along with their plan for escape.

One night his fellow prisoners helped him climb over the prison wall. He managed to get to the Appian Way where he began to flee from the city. But when he was about two miles outside the city, he met a man walking in the opposite direction. Immediately Peter recognized it was Jesus, the risen Christ. At first he was speechless, transfixed by his Lord's intense gaze. Finally, he broke the silence, "Domine, quo vadis . . . Lord, where are You going?" "I'm going to Rome to be crucified again," came the reply.

"Weren't You already crucified once for all?" Peter asked.

"Yes," Jesus answered, "but because you fled from death, I am going to be crucified in your place."

"Lord," Peter responded immediately, "I'm going back to obey Your command."

"Fear not, for I am with you," Jesus assured him, as He vanished from Peter's sight.

Then Peter retraced his steps, surrendered himself to the prison keepers, and was returned to his cell. Later he was tried and sentenced to death by crucifixion. As Jesus had predicted, his hands were stretched out—extended upon the transverse bar of a cross. But according to tradition, Peter was not crucified like Jesus was. At his own request he was crucified upside down, because he felt he was unworthy to die as his Lord had.

"You will go where you do not want to go." Jesus spoke this word to Peter and He speaks it to us today. It is another essential word about the nature of ministry. Authentic Christian ministry which flows out of love for Christ, and issues in feeding His sheep, also involves taking up the cross. Henri Nouwen says it well, "To grow in the Spirit of your Lord means to be led to the same powerless place where He was led: Calvary, the cross. It means the road of downward mobility in the midst of an upwardly mobile world."[2]

The Shape of the Cross in Ministry

The life of a minister is a cruciform life. You will go where you do not want to go. But what is the particular shape of the cross in ministry today? There is no uniform answer to that question. The cruciform life takes many shapes and forms.

1. Sometimes we encounter the cross when we take a courageous stand for the truth of the Gospel.

Several years ago I flew one Saturday evening in February to a city where I was to conduct a workshop for pastors and laity. The pastor who was the coordinator of the event met me at the airport and drove me to a motel where I was to spend the night. He was cordial and polite, but I soon sensed something was bothering him. He seemed tense, anxious, preoccupied.

The next morning I attended Sunday School and worship at the church where he had been senior pastor for only seven months. Prior to that, he had served as a district superintendent in his denomination. It was a large established downtown church, a typical "Old First Church" congregation. The membership was sophisticated, well educated, and affluent, and included several of the city's most prominent citizens.

That afternoon we drove to the conference retreat center where the event was to be held. Along the way, he told me about the explosive situation he was dealing with at the church.

A couple of months after he came to the church, an African-American man and his family began to attend. This man was a seminary graduate and had formerly been a pastor himself. Now he was working for a business firm in the city.

He and his family enjoyed the worship services and felt comfortable in the congregation. So after attending a few months, they requested that their membership be transferred there. The pastor was glad they wanted to join the church—he believed in an inclusive Gospel and wanted the congregation to reflect this. So he wrote their former church requesting a letter of transfer, and then informed them of the date when they would be received into membership.

But the pastor was not naive. He was aware of the intense racial prejudice of some of the church's influential members. They would be deeply disturbed when they found out this particular family was joining the church. The church had never had African-American members before.

So several weeks before the Sunday when they were to be received, he met with the Staff-Parish Relations Committee in order to prepare them for what was going to happen. "I think we should rejoice that this family wants to join our church," he told the committee. "In Christ we are one, regardless of race. But I realize that some people in the church will be upset. I need you to help bring them on board with what we are going to do."

The committee appeared to be unanimously in support of the pastor, and said they would encourage the members of the congregation to welcome the family into their fellowship. The pastor was pleased at their response, and confident that with the committee's help, conflict over this family joining the church would be kept to a minimum.

How shocked he was the day after the family joined the church, when that same committee met behind his back and voted unanimously to ask the district superintendent for an immediate change of pastors. In twenty-five years of ministry he had never had anything like this happen to him before. He was shaken to his foundations.

I now understood why he appeared tense and preoccupied. When he picked me up at the airport, he was still reeling from the shock of what had happened. I later learned that although he had been able to complete his first year as pastor of the church, he had moved somewhere else after that.

Sometimes this is the shape of the cross in our ministries. We stand for the truth of the Gospel. We call into question deeply rooted prejudices, cherished cultural assumptions. We confront established citadels of power. We challenge the status quo and we pay a heavy price in return. We are attacked, persecuted, betrayed, driven out.

2. But ministers encounter the cross not only when they stand for the truth of the Gospel; they also encounter it in the hostility and criticism they endure in the daily grind of ministry. According to Marshall Shelley, the amount of hostility and criticism leveled against pastors has increased in recent years. In his article, "The Problems of Battered Pastors," which he wrote after spending a year researching the positive and negative dynamics at work in churches, he described the plight of a growing number of clergy. As one pastor put it, "The constant struggle with personal attacks

and put-downs has drained me of enthusiasm. I feel like I'm bleeding to death."[3]

Shelley attributes the increase of hostility toward pastors to expanding and more demanding expectations of the minister's role. In spite of the current stress on lay ministry and the priesthood of all believers, church members still have very definite ideas about what a pastor should do. Pierce Harris describes the multiplicity of the pastoral role:

> The modern preacher has to make as many visits as a country doctor, shake as many hands as a politician, prepare as many briefs as a lawyer, and see as many people as a specialist. He has to be as good an executive as the president of a university, as good a financier as a bank president; and in the midst of it all, he has to be so good a diplomat that he could umpire a baseball game between the Knights of Columbus and the Ku Klux Klan.[4]

Of course, no one member of a congregation has all these expectations, but the composite picture, the expectations of all the members put together, which only ministers and their families see, can be overwhelming.

The basis for judging ministers has also changed. Before the advent of Christian mass media, pastors might be compared to their predecessors or other pastors in the community; now they are compared to Robert Schuller, Charles Stanley, or James Kennedy. I remember when a member of a church I was pastoring in New Jersey returned home after visiting Schuller's Crystal Cathedral in Garden Grove, California. As she filed out of the sanctuary after worship the following Sunday, she handed me their Sunday bulletin. I wanted to say to her, "When you were at the Crystal Cathedral, did you give Robert Schuller one of our bulletins?"

While expectations for ministers have both heightened and expanded, the ministerial office is diminishing in authority and prestige in American culture. We are fast becoming a Rodney Dangerfield profession—we get no respect. Pastors are in a double bind. They are expected to do more, but are given less authority to do it. The result is an increase in hostility and criticism, a cross that is increasingly heavy and difficult to bear.

3. Then there is the cross which is a part of growth. For growth involves change, and change is never without pain. Longtime members perceive newcomers as a threat to their established power. Baby boomers view the world differently than those who lived through the Great Depression. Their preference in worship style and their ways of handling money are distinct from the older generation.

The "pioneers" who first settled the area resent it when "homesteaders" arrive on the scene. They are suspicious of their strange ways and practices. "We never did it that way before!" As a result, ministers find themselves between the trenches, being shot at from both sides as two opposing factions fire away at each other.

Or, perhaps you've been called to lead a congregation

like the one Moses had. At some point in their history, because of fear or lack of vision, your people turned back from a great opportunity, from a promised land God had set before them. As a result, they are wandering in the wilderness, going in circles, making no progress. As they wander, they grumble and complain about everything; they challenge your leadership at every turn. Nevertheless, it's your job to lead them, even though they will never enter the land of promise. You have glimpsed that land, and occasionally you're allowed to climb up on the mountain and look into it. But you know the people will never enter it—at least, not while you are their leader.

Sometime in the future there may be another promised land opportunity, and a Joshua may come and lead them into it. But you're not that Joshua. You've been called to be a Moses, to bear with the unbelief and disobedience, the murmuring and ingratitude of the people. What a cross is that!

4. The cross in ministry can also take the form of financial sacrifice. At a retreat I was leading, a pastor who had previously worked as a mail carrier became very emotional as he spoke about his teenage daughter's response when he told her they couldn't afford some new clothes she wanted. " 'I wish you hadn't become a pastor,' she said, 'I wish you were still working for the post office. Then we'd have the money.' It hurt me to tell her we couldn't afford the clothes, but it hurt even more to hear her say that. Yet what could I tell her? She was right—we could have afforded

them if I was still a mail carrier."

There is a financial price to be paid for being in the ministry. No doubt about it. Most of us were aware of that when we became ministers, and so it was a freely chosen sacrifice. But what about our spouses and children? Often they had no choice in the matter. How painful then to see them suffer on our account, to be unable to provide for them as we would like to.

The cross takes a variety of shapes and forms in ministry. There are many others we could have mentioned. But the point is that if you are in Christian ministry, the cross is part of your job description. You can't escape it. You will go where you do not want to go.

How God Is Glorified

But what should be our attitude toward the cross? Should we grudgingly resign ourselves to it? Should we say sadly, "Too bad, this is just the way the ministry is. You'd better get used to it, grin and bear it, accept it, cope with it the best way you can"?

By no means. Remember, immediately following Christ's prediction concerning Peter, there is a parenthesis in the text where John interprets His words for us, "Jesus said this to indicate the kind of death by which Peter would *glorify* God" (21:19). Did you catch it? The cross—you will go where you do not want to go—this is how Peter and how we *glorify God.*

We shouldn't be surprised, because this is how Jesus glorified God. In John's Gospel, immediately following the account of the Triumphal Entry (12:12-19), some Greeks attending the Passover festival come to the disciples requesting an audience with Jesus. This confirms what the Pharisees had said, "Look how the whole world has gone after Him" (12:19).

But when Jesus is made aware of their request, does He agree to meet with them? No. Instead He declares, "The hour has come for the Son of man to be glorified. I tell you the truth, unless a kernel of wheat falls to the ground and dies, it remains only a single seed. But if it dies, it produces many seeds" (12:23-24). Jesus was glorified not by crowds shouting Hosanna and waving palm branches, not by the world going after Him, but through His death on the cross.

In the same way, God is glorified through the cross borne by Christ's disciples. This is how they too bear much fruit (see John 15:8) and how God's work is accomplished. As we die to self, as we take up the cross, God's presence is made manifest and God's power is let loose in the world. Out of death comes life, out of defeat comes victory, out of sorrow comes joy. "If it dies, it bears much fruit."

Dennis Kinlaw, former president of Asbury College, saw this principle powerfully at work in a member of a church he was pastoring many years ago. When he began to serve the church, he found few in the congregation with much spiritual vitality or depth. Most of the members were nominal Christians. But there was one woman, a teacher of an adult Sunday School class, who had a vibrant, dynamic faith.

She loved Christ with all her heart and was striving to live totally for Him.

Several years before, when she became a member of the church, she too was only a nominal Christian. The church was in desperate need of Sunday School teachers at the time, so they asked her if she would take an adult class. She reluctantly agreed, but then found it was something she enjoyed doing. She was conscientious in preparing her lessons, and as a result, for the first time in her life she was giving serious attention to the Scriptures. One day while she was studying the Bible, God's written Word, she came face-to-face with Jesus Christ, the living Word, and her life was transformed.

But as she began then to teach her Sunday School class, no longer from secondhand, theoretical knowledge of Christ, but from firsthand experience of what He was doing in her life, some of the members of that class began to find her offensive. Her vibrant, dynamic faith was an indictment on their nominalism and it made them uncomfortable. They had been members of the church much longer than she. What right did she have to speak to them as if there was something lacking in their faith? Their resentment toward her grew until finally they began to circulate a petition around the church to get rid of her as the teacher of their class.

When Dr. Kinlaw heard about the petition, he was deeply dismayed. "Lord," he sighed, "she's the best we've got. Why would they circulate a petition to get rid of her?"

Later when he visited her, they sat at her kitchen table and talked about what had happened. "Dennis," she said sadly, "all my life I've been searching for God. Now I've found Him. I'm also in a church where I am growing in my faith and I have an opportunity to serve. But now this happens. What should I do? I guess I'll have to leave the church."

"Not so fast," Kinlaw responded. "Why do you have to do that?"

"Well, I can't go back where they don't want me," she replied.

"But maybe that's exactly where you need to go," he said. In encouraging her to stay, Kinlaw wasn't sure of his own motives. Was that God's will for her, or was he just being a possessive pastor who didn't want to lose a valuable church member?

The woman was surprised at his suggestion. "You wouldn't ask me to go back into a church that had circulated a petition to get rid of me."

"No, I wouldn't," Kinlaw assured her. "But think about what happened to Jesus. When He taught, the religious people didn't want Him either. There are folks in this congregation who need Christ and need your witness. How can you leave now?"

"But, Dennis," she responded. "What about Tom?" Her husband, Tom, was one of the roughest characters Kinlaw had ever met. One day in speaking to Kinlaw about one of the church officers who had been pestering him about coming to church, he shook his fist and vowed, "If that man says another word to me about coming to church, I'll mop the middle aisle of the sanctuary with him." And he would have—he was that kind of person.

"Right now Tom is ready to tear everybody at the church apart limb by limb. I can't go back there the way he is."

But Kinlaw kept pressing, "Don't be so sure. Maybe you ought to."

"You mean you'd have me walk back in there and sit down in that Sunday School class while somebody else teaches in my place?"

"Maybe that's what you need to do. But if you do it, don't be judgmental or act spiritually superior. I wonder, can you just go and sit there and lovingly pray for the person who has taken your place?"

"You couldn't ask me to do that!"

"No. But what if *Jesus* were to ask you to do that?"

She wept and agonized as they continued talking. Then they prayed together about the situation. He left her home, not knowing what she would do—nor what she should do.

But the next Sunday morning, there she was sitting in the class, quietly praying for the teacher who had taken her place and for those in the class who had opposed her. She had decided to take up the cross. What she liked or what made her comfortable wasn't important anymore. She had come to the place where she was willing to say, "Lord, even if it's a cup of bitterness, I'll take it if it's what You want."

One morning a few weeks later when Dr. Kinlaw drove

into the church parking lot, the man whom Tom was going
to mop the middle aisle of the sanctuary with was there
waiting for him. "Dennis, Dennis," he exclaimed, "have you
heard about Tom?"

From the look on the man's face, Kinlaw braced himself
for some bad news. He thought perhaps Tom had been in
an accident. "No, what is it?" he asked.

"I was just with him. Tom says he received Christ last
night."

"You've got to be kidding. Where is he?"

"He's at home, and he wants to talk to you."

Kinlaw got back in his car, and drove off to see Tom.
When he found him, he shook his hand and said, "Tom,
what's happened to you?"

"Oh, Dennis," he said excitedly, "last night I found Christ."

'How did you do that, Tom?" Kinlaw inquired. "There
aren't any revival meetings going on around here!"

"No, but living with my wife lately has been like living
with one! When this church problem first came up, I said to
her, 'If you'll just let me, I'll go up there and straighten
every one of those people out.' But I listened to her pray,
and she prayed so lovingly for them that finally I couldn't
take it any longer. I said to her, 'Don't just pray for *them*.
They don't need it nearly as much as I do. Pray for *me* too.'
And last night in our bedroom, I asked Christ to come into
my life."

"Unless a kernel of wheat falls to the ground and dies, it
remains only a single seed. But if it dies, it produces many

seeds" (John 12:24). Out of her death to self came new life. Out of her willingness to bear the cross, God was glorified. God's presence was manifest in such power that her husband's heart melted, his defenses shattered. He too came to know the living Christ.

Paul states the same principle which he saw at work throughout his life and ministry, "We always carry around in our body the death of Jesus, so that the life of Jesus may also be revealed in our body" (2 Corinthians 4:10). When we take up the cross, God is glorified. The divine presence is made manifest through sacrifice and self-denial.

Someone Else Will Carry You

"You will go where you do not want to go." If you are faithful in ministry, you cannot avoid the cross. As you walk with Christ, you too will find yourself on the road to Calvary. Your ministry, like His, will be cruciform.

Don't shy away from the cross or seek to avoid it. This is how God's kingdom work is accomplished. Through the cross, God is glorified and His power and presence are made manifest. So endure it not with bitter resignation, but, as Jesus did, "for the joy set before Him" (Hebrews 12:2).

"You will go where you do not want to go." Jesus speaks this essential word about Christian ministry to Peter and to us. It is not a popular word, not one we are eager to hear, and so it is often overlooked. John Stott sums it up well:

The place of suffering in service and passion in mission is hardly ever taught today. But the greatest single secret of evangelistic or missionary effectiveness is the willingness to suffer and die. It may be a death to popularity (by faithfully preaching the unpopular biblical Gospel), or to pride (by the use of modest methods in reliance on the Holy Spirit), or to racial and national prejudice (by identification with another culture), or to material comfort (by adopting a simple lifestyle). But the servant must suffer if he is to bring light to the nations, and the seed must die if it is to multiply.[5]

But Christ's prediction also contains a promise, *"Someone else* will dress you and lead you where you do not want to go" (John 21:18). Who is the "someone else"? Obviously those who will inflict the cross upon Peter. But the "someone else" is also the risen Christ Himself! As God spoke to Israel, so Christ speaks to us, "Even to your old age and gray hairs I am He, I am He who will sustain you. I have made you and I will carry you" (Isaiah 46:4).

Christ who makes the prediction is the One who fulfills it in us. *He* takes us where we do not want to go. As we abide in Him and He abides in us, the same disposition of self-sacrifice which caused Him to say, "Not My will, but Yours be done" (Luke 22:42), is made manifest in us. By His presence in us we are drawn toward the cross.

As a result, the cross we bear in ministry is not burdensome. It *is* a burden, but it is not heavy because Jesus Himself bears it in us and through us. And as He promised, His yoke is easy and His burden is light (Matthew 11:30).

He never commands us to do anything without He Himself providing the power to do what He commands. So we go where we do not want to go, not in our own strength but in His. His commands are His enablings. "The One who calls you is faithful, and He will do it" (1 Thessalonians 5:24).

Chapter Four
Follow Me

The working minister is in a co-working ministry day after day with Christ's own ministry, supported and energized by the Holy Spirit.

Thomas Oden

Jesus has just told Peter he will die an unnatural death. He will go where he does not want to go. Those were not easy words for Peter to hear, and we will see how he responds to them in the next chapter.

But before he can respond, Jesus speaks again, saying to Peter, "Follow Me" (John 21:19).

"Follow Me." Peter has heard those words before. They were among the first words Jesus ever spoke to him. He heard them the day Jesus called him to leave his nets to come fish for people. Memories of that day must have flooded his mind. Now Peter, by the same lakeshore, hears the words again.

Yet it isn't the same. So much has happened since that day. How sure of himself, how naive and foolish he was then. Not anymore. Now he is paralyzed by pessimism and self-doubt. His disgraceful failure has forced him to face his dark side. What a spineless, self-protecting coward he turned out to be!

Peter had emphatically insisted, "Even if I have to die with You, I will never disown You" (Mark 14:31). Now Jesus predicted that one day Peter would, in fact, die on a cross as He had. Through Peter's death God would be glorified.

But how? What would prevent Peter from disowning Jesus then, just as he had a few days before? Cocksure Peter had heard the cock crow. He had remembered what Jesus said about denial, and he had wept bitterly. The only thing he was sure of now was how unsure he was of himself!

But now the call of Christ comes to him again, "Follow Me." This was the same call he heard three years before, but it was different too. For not only was Peter a different person; so was Jesus! The One who was calling him to follow had been raised from the dead. The scars on His hands and feet and side were radiant scars!

"Follow Me." Now it was the call of the risen Christ. It was a call in the light of the empty tomb, in the light of Easter. And what a difference that day had made!

This time it was not a call to follow in the footsteps of a mere man, one of many Jewish rabbis he could pattern his life after. Peter had tried that for three years and had failed miserably. This time it was a call to participate in the ongoing life and ministry of the One who was alive forevermore. "Follow *Me.*"

Jesus' prediction had contained a promise, "*Someone else* will lead you where you do not want to go." That someone else was the risen Christ Himself. Now the call to follow came from Him. He was no longer limited by a human body. He had conquered sin and death and hell. He was alive!

"Follow Me." By calling Peter again Jesus was saying, "I will continue to go before you, Peter. I will not be with you as I was before I was crucified. I will no longer be physically present with you, but My ministry is not over. It's only just begun! I am alive forevermore! No longer am I limited by space and time. Now I can minister as never before. Your calling, Peter, is to follow Me. It's not your responsibility to lead now or to carry on the work I began. I will go before you. You are called to join Me in My ongoing ministry and to let Me carry out that ministry though you."

Participating in Christ's Ministry

"Follow Me." Jesus' call to Peter reminds us of a basic fact of ministry we so easily forget: the ministry is not primarily *ours* but *His.* Our ministry is a participation in the ministry of Christ.

I wish I had had a better grasp of this fact when I began pastoring. Because I didn't, I assumed I was the principal actor in ministry. It was *my* ministry and it was up to me to make it happen. Of course, Jesus was the center of the Gospel I had been called to proclaim—I understood that right—but it was my ministry. I was to offer Christ to others.

After pastoring about five years, I read James Smart's *The Rebirth of Ministry*. Smart challenged me to rethink my conception of ministry. I was struck by statements of his such as these:

> The essential nature of the Christian ministry has been determined for all time by the ministry of Jesus Christ. All our thinking must take His person and ministry as its starting point.[1]

> The ministry into which we enter is the ministry *of Jesus Christ*. We are not free to determine its nature as we will; its nature has already been determined for us by His life, death, and resurrection, and by the work of His Spirit in the shaping of the apostolic ministry.[2]

> The apostolic ministry, then, in which the Christian ministry received its decisive formulation is simply the ministry of Jesus Christ being continued, expanded, and carried ever farther afield in the world as Jesus Christ lives and speaks and acts redemptively through His ministers.[3]

As I reflected on the implications of what Smart was saying, I realized that all authentic Christian ministry is a participation in the ongoing ministry of the risen Christ. We are to follow Him as he continues His ministry in the world.

The words of Luke at the very beginning of Acts took on new meaning. "In my former book" he states, "I wrote about all that Jesus began to do and to teach until the day He was taken up to heaven" (Acts 1:1-2). By the phrase "began to do and to teach," Luke is implying that even following His death and resurrection Jesus continues to do and to teach, and that in this book he is going to set forth an account of the ongoing acts of Jesus.

Thus, Jesus' ministry did not end when He ascended to the Father. It merely assumed a different shape. Through His body, the church, the ministry of Jesus continues. We are an extension of His incarnation. And if this holds true for the general ministry into which all Christians are baptized and called, doesn't it especially hold true for the representative ministry to which pastors have been ordained?

First and foremost then, Christian ministry is an extension of Christ's ministry. It is not so much asking Him to join me in my ministry as I offer Him to others. Rather, it is joining Him in His ongoing ministry as He offers Himself to others through me.

Understanding this has changed the way I pray. As I approach various aspects of ministry, I find myself praying less, "Lord, help me," and more, "Lord, help Yourself to me." In the past, for example, when I approached a worship service, I would pray, "Lord, help me to lead well and preach well so You will be glorified." Now I pray, "Lord, what do You want to do in this service? Help me not to stand in the way of that. Help Yourself to me. Use me to accomplish Your purposes." Before, my concern was to ask Christ to bless my ministry. Now, my concern is not to be an obstacle to His ministry, but an instrument He can use in accomplishing it.

I have found this understanding of ministry to be tremendously liberating, for it relieves me of the burden of ministry. I don't have to *make* it happen. My task is to *let* it happen. The battle is the *Lord's,* not mine. This doesn't mean I don't work or take preparation seriously. I do. But the pressure is off me. I am not the one who is ultimately responsible for the outcome—Christ is.

So much burnout among pastors today is a direct result of our failure to understand this. We are carrying a burden Christ never intended for us to carry: the burden of having to make ministry happen. It is a burden too heavy for anyone to bear. No wonder we collapse under its weight.

Christ's yoke is easy and His burden is light. He invites us into the freedom and rest of knowing that the outcome of ministry is ultimately in His hands, not ours. Our job is not to lead but to follow the Leader, our risen Lord, as He ministers to His body and the world, and then to encourage our congregation to follow Him too.

This doesn't mean that our work and preparation is not important. It is. But it changes our approach to it. I recall, for example, the advice I was given in seminary about preaching, "*Preach* as if everything depended on *God,* but *prepare* as if everything depended on *you.*" It was intended to cause us to take sermon preparation seriously and counter the naive notion that preaching is primarily the result of direct divine inspiration which occurs when one enters the pulpit on Sunday.

I took that advice to heart, and I'm glad I did. If preaching is to make an impact for God, there is no substitute for thoroughly disciplined sermon preparation. As my conception of the ministry has changed, my commitment to preparation has remained firm.

But my approach to preparation has changed. I would reword the advice I was given in seminary to, "*Preach* as if everything depended on *God* and *prepare* as if everything depended on *God.*" Preparing as if everything depends on God doesn't mean you don't prepare! It means you go about it differently than when everything depends on you.

Prayer becomes more important both prior to putting the sermon together and during the actual preparation of it. I may be meditating on a text, studying commentaries, struggling to get an outline, looking for illustrations, or pondering the wording of a sentence, but throughout it all I am praying, "Lord, You want to speak to Your people through me. What is it You want to say? I open my heart and mind to You. Speak to Your servant. Use me to speak Your Word."

I prepare diligently, but no longer is the burden of preparation on me. I don't have to "come up with" a sermon. The pressure is off. Christ is the Head of the church and He longs to speak to His people. I will never be able to exhaust all the sermons He wants to preach to them! In all facets of my preparation, my task is to be attentive to Christ's voice, to hear Him speaking through His Word, so that I can convey what He is saying to His body.

Charles Spurgeon, the great nineteenth-century prince of the pulpit, had a profound grasp of this. Every Sunday there were 6,000 people in his congregation. For many years his sermons were cabled from London to New York every Monday and reprinted in leading American newspapers. He occupied the same pulpit for almost forty years without repeating himself or preaching himself dry. How did he do it? Here is how Helmut Thielicke, another great preacher, described Spurgeon's secret:

> He worked only through the power of the Word which created its own hearers and changed souls.
>
> Now this was not *his* word, the product of his own rhetorical skills. It was rather a word which he himself had "merely" heard. He put himself at its disposal, as a mere echo, and it brought to him the Spirit over whom he did not himself dispose. His message never ran dry because he was never anything but a recipient.
>
> Nor did he live spiritually beyond his means. For he gave only what flowed into him in never-ceasing supply from the channels of Holy Scripture. With pails and buckets he went up even the remotest rills

and tributaries of the stream to bring water to the thirsty, and to make fruitful the land of barren souls.[4]

Understanding that I am to follow Christ in His ongoing ministry has also increased my confidence and boldness in ministering to people. On the first Easter, the angel said to the women at the tomb, "Go, tell His disciples and Peter, 'He is going ahead of you into Galilee. There you will see Him, just as He told you' " (Mark 16:7). That promise was partly fulfilled in Christ's lakeside appearance to the disciples and His conversation with Peter which we have been considering. But it is also a promise for us. Jesus goes before us too! No matter where we are, He has gone ahead of us and is at work in the situation and the lives of the people. We are never the first witness to Christ in a person's life. Nor is it our task to bring Christ to a situation. He is already there! He has gone before us and has prepared the way. Knowing this enables us to approach ministry with greater confidence—not because we are confident in ourselves, but because we are confident in what He is doing.

I was counseling the wife of a seminary student. As she began to tell me the tangled, sordid story of her life, I was overwhelmed. There was so much pain, so many problems and issues to deal with. I prayed, "Lord, I don't have a clue as to where to begin. But You've been working in her life. Come now and manifest Your presence in our midst."

I can't remember what I said, what questions I asked, or even if I said anything, but before I knew it, Jesus had

answered my prayer. He came into the situation, revealed
to her where she needed to begin, and began to minister
His healing grace to her. She left my office praising God for
what He had done for her.

I sat there shaking my head, in awe at what had taken
place. "Lord," I said, "how did that happen? I didn't do
anything!"

"Yes, you did," He seemed to whisper. "You made yourself available to Me. You invited Me to come, and you didn't
stand in the way when I did." Then my eyes fell on a piece
of paper on my desk on which I had scribbled a statement
of Oswald Chambers about ministry: "Go to Jesus and say,
'Lord, these people want to see You.' Rely on the Holy
Spirit to help you. Live among the facts of God's Word and
among human facts, so that people will recognize Jesus
Christ through you."[5]

The key to fruitful ministry is to be so open and available
to the risen Christ that He is free to manifest Himself in the
situation. He has gone before us. He is already there. Now
His presence needs to be made manifest. When we do this,
whatever needs to happen in a situation will happen!

Co-laboring with Christ in Prayer

I have touched briefly upon several aspects of my ministry
which have been affected by understanding ministry as par-
ticipating in Christ's ministry. Now I would like to describe
in more detail how it has affected a crucial aspect of ministry which I had tended to neglect: intercessory prayer.

When the apostles were faced with administrative problems resulting from the growth of the church, they delegated those responsibilities to others so that they could give "attention to prayer and the ministry of the Word" (Acts 6:4). Recognizing that prayer was central to their calling, they devoted themselves to it. It could not be delegated to anyone else. Along with the ministry of the Word, prayer took priority over everything else.

Years ago I knew that prayer was an essential part of my calling, and that a major part of my time spent in prayer should involve intercession for the needs and concerns of others. So I made sure a portion of my prayertime was devoted to it. I prayed for my family and friends, I prayed for our nation, I prayed for the worldwide advance of the Gospel. When I was a pastor, I prayed for the church I was serving and the individual members of the congregation. Now as a seminary professor, I pray for my students and the institution where I teach.

Yet I must confess that most of the time, my time spent in intercession for others was done halfheartedly and mostly out of a sense of duty. I knew I should do it, so I did. But I found it much easier to pray for myself than for others. My enthusiasm for intercession was generally low.

However, as I've begun to approach intercession with the intention of joining Christ in His ministry, my attitude toward it has changed. True intercession is simply a participation in the ongoing intercession of the risen and ascended Christ. Having ascended into heaven where He is at the

Father's right hand, the exalted Christ is now engaged in the ongoing work of intercession. Paul declares it, "Christ Jesus, who died—more than that, who was raised to life—is at the right hand of God and is also interceding for us" (Romans 8:34). Likewise, the writer of Hebrews states that Jesus our eternal High Priest "always lives to intercede" for us (Hebrews 7:25).

Christ, then, is the principal actor in intercession. The burden of intercession is not *ours*, but *His*. "Unless He intercedes," said Ambrose, "there is no intercourse with God, either for us or for all saints."[6] Consequently, we are not called to bear the burden of intercession but to "piggyback" upon His intercession, to be co-laborers with Him in His ongoing intercession in heaven.

Some years ago this truth came home to me in a dramatic way. In May 1990, I was in Ypsilanti, Michigan on the campus of Eastern Michigan University attending two conferences for pastors and Christian leaders being held concurrently. Fifteen hundred people were gathered in the gymnasium the first evening of the conferences for a time of worship and ministry. John Wimber from the Vineyard Christian Fellowship was leading the service. After he preached, scores of people responded to his invitation. When they had gathered at the front, Wimber began to pray.

I was sitting between my father and a close friend, intently observing what was happening, sensing God's presence in our midst. At some point in his prayer Wimber said,

"Now, Lord, let the spirit of intercession fall upon Your people." The farthest thing from my mind that evening was the seminary where I teach. One of my reasons for attending the conference was to *get away* from the seminary and the end of semester busyness. But as soon as he prayed those words, I found myself thinking about the seminary and particularly the conflict among our faculty over a particular issue related to institutional growth.

Before I knew it there were tears in my eyes. I wasn't just thinking about the situation, I was crying about it. And then, I found myself not only crying, but crying out so loudly that people all around could hear me. There was such a deep groaning within I couldn't contain myself. "O God," I kept crying. "O God." And I couldn't stop. The groaning and the crying went on for several minutes.

When I finally quieted down, the Lord seemed to whisper to me, "Steve, I know the conflict at the seminary is upsetting you, but you have no idea how it is upsetting Me. It's breaking My heart."

A few days after I returned from the conference, I was talking with several faculty colleagues. They were expressing their concern about a faculty meeting I had missed while attending the conference. During that meeting the underlying conflict had erupted again. I took a deep breath and said, "Can I tell you about something that happened to me recently?" Then with considerable hesitation, not sure of what they would think of my off-the-wall experience, I described what had happened to me that evening at the conference. When I had finished, they all seemed to be taken aback. Then I said, "Since that conference, God has placed a burden upon my heart to pray for our situation. Would you like to join with me next week for a time of intercessory prayer for the seminary?"

They all agreed, and so seven of us got together and prayed for over an hour. We didn't analyze the problem or propose solutions—something seminary professors are so good at—we simply prayed about it. Like King Jehoshaphat in the face of the vast enemy army, we were at the point where all we could say was, "We do not know what to do, but our eyes are upon You" (2 Chronicles 20:12).

Over the summer months, I went to about twenty other faculty members, told them about my experience, and invited them to join us for prayer at what became a monthly faculty intercessory prayer meeting which continued for the next two years. In the fall we witnessed a major breakthrough in relation to the conflict which had torn our community. We still bear some scars, but since that breakthrough the situation has been significantly altered.

What I experienced that evening brought the reality of Christ's intercession home to me in a forceful way. In reflecting on what happened, I realized that as I cried out, I was caught up in something much bigger than I was, in something I hadn't initiated. For a few moments, I experienced a measure of the intensity of Christ's intercession. In some mysterious way, I was caught up in the intercession of the Son at the Father's right hand.

Of course, I don't usually experience the reality of Christ's intercession in such a dramatic fashion. Often when I intercede for others, I *feel* very little, but that doesn't discourage me as it once might have. Realizing that my intercession is a participation in Christ's intercession, I find myself simply inviting Jesus to pray in me and through me for that particular person or situation. I also invite the Holy Spirit to come as the Spirit of intercession to show me how to pray for others and then to pray in me on their behalf (Romans 8:26-27). And He does!

Too often we take the burden of intercession upon ourselves, as if we have to make it happen. We feel guilty because we don't care enough and pray enough for others. "Lord," we plead, "help me to pray more for so and so." When we realize that we are called to intercede *with* Him rather than *for* Him, the burden is no longer heavy but light.

Amy Carmichael, who worked among the temple girls of South India, told about a time when the opposition to her work grew so intense and the evil which bound the girls seemed so strong that she wondered if she could carry the burden any longer:

> At last a day came when the burden grew too heavy for me; and then it was as though the tamarind trees about the house were not tamarind, but olive, and under one of these trees our Lord Jesus knelt alone. And I knew that this was His burden, not mine. It

was He who was asking me to share it with Him, not I who was asking Him to share it with me. After that there was only one thing to do; who that saw Him kneeling there could turn away and forget? Who could have done anything but go into the garden and kneel down beside Him under the olive trees?[7]

Christ is looking for those who will join Him in His great work of intercession. Realizing this has changed my whole attitude toward intercession. What a privilege it is to be able to join Him!

The Shape of Christ's Ongoing Ministry

Understanding that our ministry is a participation in the ongoing ministry of Christ changes the nature of it. It places the emphasis where it needs to be—on Him, not on us. It also indicates what the shape of our ministry should be.

In Philippians 2:5-11, that great Christological passage which many scholars believe was an early Christian hymn, Paul outlines for us the three major "movements" in the life and ministry of Christ. These movements ought to be seen in our ministries as well. So let's consider them and reflect upon their implications for us.

1. Incarnation. "Who, being in very nature God, did not consider equality with God something to be grasped, but made Himself nothing, taking the very nature of a servant, being made in human likeness" (vv. 6-7).

Christ Jesus, the Divine Word, became flesh and dwelt

among us. He identified with us fully in our humanity. He experienced our human limitations. He shared in our guilt and our suffering. He is Emmanuel—God in it with us all the way, eyeball to eyeball, heart to heart.

Through this first movement, incarnation, we learn of God's love for and affirmation of His creation. For by assuming the likeness of sinful flesh (Romans 8:3), by joining Himself to fallen humanity, God is saying, "Even though you are sinful and fallen, I choose not to reject you. I affirm you. I join Myself to you. I haven't given up on you. I declare you are redeemable."

2. Crucifixion. "And being found in appearance as a man, He humbled Himself and became obedient to death— even death on a cross!" (v. 8)

Jesus identified with us all the way to the point of a shameful, violent death on a cross. He was wounded for our transgressions and bruised for our iniquities. He bore our sufferings and infirmities. He bore the guilt and the curse of sin.

Through this second movement, crucifixion, we learn of God's judgment on creation. On the cross Jesus cried out, "My God, My God, why have You forsaken Me?" (Mark 15:34) In His God-forsakenness, He experienced God's condemnation on the fallen human race. As Dietrich Bonhoeffer explains, "The rejection of God on the cross of Jesus Christ contains within itself the rejection of the whole human race. The cross of Jesus is the death sentence upon the world."[8]

3. Resurrection. "Therefore God exalted Him to the

highest place and gave Him the name that is above every name, that at the name of Jesus every knee should bow" (vv. 9-10).

Jesus, the One who was sentenced and condemned by God, is also the One God raised to new life. God's love for creation is therefore stronger than death. Through the miracle of resurrection, God re-creates. The old has passed away, all things have become new. Through Christ's resurrection a new creation emerges.

In this third movement, resurrection, we learn of God's will for the world. He desires to make all things new. In the midst of the old world of decay and death, resurrection has dawned as a living reality to be experienced now and a promise of the future when there will be a new heaven and a new earth, when all things will be made new.

The Application of Christ's Ongoing Ministry

These then are the three major movements in the ministry of Christ: incarnation, crucifixion, resurrection. They are so central to our faith that the major seasons of the church year—Advent, Lent, and Easter—revolve around them. We can summarize their meaning, by describing incarnation as affirmation, crucifixion as condemnation, and resurrection as re-creation.

My purpose, however, in outlining these major movements in Christ's ministry is not theoretical. My concern is to indicate their relevance for ministry. For if Christ's ministry is continuing in the world today, shouldn't we expect it to be taking essentially the same shape it did originally? And if our ministry is a part of the ongoing ministry of Christ, shouldn't we expect to see these three movements repeatedly played out in our life and ministry?

Reflecting upon the shape of our ministry in the light of the three movements in Christ's ministry can help us make sense of much we do as pastors. It can also serve as a criterion for evaluating what we do.

1. Incarnation. Think of all the things we do which correspond to this movement in Christ's ministry:

Loving and affirming our congregations.
Living in their communities.
Accepting them where they are.
Taking the time to get to know them.
Learning their names.
Working alongside them.
Playing with them.
Visiting in their homes.
Sharing in their joys and sorrows.
Gaining an appreciation for their culture.
Getting involved in the life of their community.
Allowing our people to get to know us.
Making ourselves vulnerable to them.
Letting them observe us in all our humanness.
Staying long enough so that all this can happen.

Christ is there living in the midst of the people, identifying with them, loving and affirming them through us. The Word becomes flesh through us.

2. Crucifixion. If we are faithful in proclaiming the Gospel, at the same time we are accepting and affirming people where they are, we will also be pronouncing judgment on them and calling them into question. For the Gospel confronts human sin in all its expressions. It reveals the extent of our alienation and rebellion against God. It commands us to repent, turn from our wickedness, die to ourselves, and submit to Christ's lordship.

The Gospel confronts not only the individual but also the community. As we present our congregations with a vision of the church based on the biblical pattern, it will stand in judgment on anything present in the church not in keeping with it.

If then we are faithful in proclaiming the Gospel, several responses are sure to follow. Some people will accept the judgment on their sinfulness and the church's sinfulness. They will repent and turn to God and receive forgiveness and new life. But others will resist and reject the Gospel. They will refuse the judgment on their sinfulness or the church's sinfulness. They will harden their hearts and refuse to repent. As a result of their rebellion they will turn against us. When they do we will experience crucifixion.

If we are partners with Christ in His ongoing ministry, we can expect to die. In fact, as we saw in the last chapter, the ministry presents us with all sorts of opportunities to die. We will go where we do not want to go.

3. Resurrection. Out of the old comes a new creation. Out of death new life emerges through the power of Christ's resurrection. Out of brokenness comes wholeness.

We witness resurrection in the lives of individuals in our congregation. As they respond to the Gospel, they experience new life in Christ and are set free from all sorts of bondage and brokenness. They discover the glorious liberty of being children of God and experience the joy of being instruments of His grace to others.

We also witness resurrection in the congregation as a whole, as it discovers what it means to be the body of Christ. There is a depth of fellowship and love for one another they have never known before. Members use their gifts in ministering to one another. The church begins to look beyond itself, catching a vision of the mission God has for it in the community and the world. The presence and power of God is manifest in gatherings for worship.

Resurrection occurs in our lives too. Out of our death, our brokenness, our despair, our defeat, Christ's resurrection power is unleashed. Paul's experience is echoed in ours, "For we who are alive are always being given over to death for Jesus' sake, so that His life may be revealed in our mortal body" (2 Corinthians 4:11).

These three major movements of the ministry of Christ will be played out in our ministries again and again. *It is important that they be kept in proper balance.* Some pastors, for example, find themselves naturally drawn to the first movement, incarnation, but neglect the second, crucifixion. They do a wonderful job of affirming their people and identifying with them where they are. But they are afraid to rock the boat. They never speak the word which judges and calls sin into question. Their love soon degenerates into sentimentality—sloppy agape.

Other pastors go to the opposite extreme. They are not afraid to confront the sins of the people. But they do it harshly, smugly, self-righteously.

Similarly, there are pastors who present the cross as God's judgment on sin, but offer no hope of resurrection, no possibility of transformation and new life. Their congregations live in a dark tunnel of guilt, confusion, and despair.

Our Primary Calling

"Follow Me." Jesus' words to Peter indicate that His ministry is the essential standard and criterion. Our ministries are most authentic when we participate in His. As Thomas Oden maintains, "If ministry cannot be clearly established as the continuation of Jesus' own intention and practice, we lose its central theological premise."[9]

Jesus' words also remind us again of our primary calling as ministers: to abide in Christ. For if we abide in Him and commune with Him as we ought, then we will know what He is doing in the world. In relation to His ministry, Jesus stressed He did nothing on His own, but only did what He saw the Father doing (John 5:19). Our ministries should follow the same pattern. We should not act on our own but should only do what we see Jesus doing.

That will happen only if we constantly abide in Him. As we abide in Him, Jesus is free to carry out His ministry through us. Abiding then is our primary business. The call, "Follow Me," sends us back to the question, "Do you love Me?" Apart from Him we can do nothing, but if we abide in Him, we will bear much fruit, because He will abide in us. His ministry will be carried out through ours. And people will take note of us, as they did the apostles, that we have been with Jesus (Acts 4:13).

Chapter Five
What Is That to You?
Follow Me!

*Envy causes us to want to be what we were
never created to be—someone else.*

Robert Schnase

eter has heard Jesus' prediction, "You will go where
you do not want to go." He has heard Him say,
"Follow Me." And how does he react? Like impul-
sive, impetuous Peter always does. The text says, "Peter
turned and saw that the disciple whom Jesus loved was
following them. . . . When Peter saw him, he asked, 'Lord,
what about him?' " (John 21:20-21)

Peter is concerned about John, the beloved disciple, the
one closest to Jesus. *How is he going to die? Is the same
thing in store for John that's in store for me? Or is he going
to receive preferential treatment?* So Peter blurts out,
"Lord, what about him?"

Jesus responds to Peter with a stern rebuke, "If I want him to remain alive until I return, what is that to you? You must follow Me" (21:22). Sensing the ill will rising in Peter, Jesus confronts him in no uncertain terms. "Peter, what's going to happen to John is none of your business. Your business is simply to follow Me."

Oh, Peter! This time you've really opened up a can of worms! Envy and jealousy among pastors . . . ministerial competitiveness . . . professional gossip and backbiting . . . has there ever been a pastor who didn't struggle with these issues?

"Lord, it's not fair. It's not right. I went where I didn't want to go. I agreed to serve this church even though I knew it wasn't a very promising place for ministry. I came because I believed You wanted me to. And now, look at so-and-so—he's moving to the church I would like to pastor, and I have some very serious questions about his motives for ministry." Haven't we all struggled with thoughts like these? Like Miriam and Aaron who were jealous of Moses' position of leadership, haven't we said concerning some other servant of God, "Has the Lord spoken only through Moses? Hasn't He also spoken through us?" (Numbers 12:2)

Ralph Turnbull's *A Minister's Obstacles* portrays the major pitfalls facing ministers. In a chapter entitled, "The Bane of Jealousy," there is a fable about a time when the devil was crossing the Libyan desert and came upon some frustrated junior devils who were tempting a saintly Desert Father. First they tempted him with lustful thoughts. That didn't work. Then they tried to fill his mind with doubts and fears about his relationship with God, but that didn't work either. Then they raised questions about the sincerity of his sacrificial lifestyle. Again they were unsuccessful.

By this time the junior devils were getting discouraged, and so the devil himself stepped in. "Your methods are much too crude," he said. "Permit me for a moment."

Approaching the Desert Father he said, "Have you heard the news? Your brother has just been made Bishop of Alexandria." Almost immediately a scowl of jealousy broke across the saintly man's face.

Envy, along with its twin sister jealousy, can be exceedingly subtle. That is why it is often found in the hearts of persons whom society considers good and respectable. Pastors may be able to stand against the grosser sins of the flesh, but they find it very difficult to resist comparing themselves to others in ministry and envying those who seem to be more effective or popular. Pilate understood clearly that this was behind the opposition of the chief priests and Pharisees to Jesus. He knew it was "out of envy that the chief priests had handed Jesus over to him" (Mark 15:10). Later their jealousy would cause them to arrest the apostles (Acts 5:17-18). Yes, envy's green eyes often glow in the ministry!

In *The Brothers Karamazov*, Dostoevsky offers a penetrating study of envy among religious people. Father Zossima was a devout man to whom scores of people came for help and guidance. But the very spirituality which drew people to him also prompted jealousy in others:

Though the late elder had won over many hearts, more by love than by miracles, and had gathered round him a mass of loving adherents, none the less, in fact, rather the more on that account he had awakened jealousy, and so had come to have bitter enemies, secret and open, not only in the monastery but in the world outside it. He did no one any harm, but "Why do they think him so saintly?" And that question alone, gradually repeated, gave rise at last to an intense, insatiable hatred of him.[1]

Envy and jealousy begin as inner attitudes, but they soon find outer expression. Brian Whitlow aptly describes the progressive ways in which they manifest themselves. They often begin with small expressions of dislike—"I just don't know why everybody raves about her." Then come innuendoes and half-truths—"There are other factors involved which I'm not at liberty to discuss." Next, questioning another's motives—"I wonder if that's the *real* reason he did it." Followed by faultfinding—"She sure messed that up, as usual." And finally out-and-out slander itself—"Have you heard about so-and-so?"[2]

The Destructive Power of Envy and Jealousy

Envy and jealousy are destructive to our spirits in so many ways. Proverbs 14:30 says it well, "A heart at peace gives life to the body, but envy rots the bones." Think of how these poisonous attitudes isolate us from one another. Instead of looking upon other pastors as co-laborers in the Gospel, colleagues in the ministry of Christ, we view them as competitors. Their success threatens us, and we find ourselves playing one-upmanship games with them. As a result we can never risk being open with them about our needs and struggles, for then we would appear weak. So we hide our true selves and pretend everything is all right. We bear our burdens all alone.

A pastor friend of mine related how he felt the sting of jealousy while attending his denomination's annual conference. Prior to conference, it had been announced that he was going to be moving to a larger church—one with considerable potential for ministry. He was well deserving of the appointment, for he had served his present church faithfully and had the gifts for effective ministry in the church where he was being sent. The bishop was to make the appointment official at the conference.

"I was looking forward to attending conference," he said to me, "particularly the times of fellowship with other pastors. But this was without a doubt the loneliest annual conference I've ever experienced. I couldn't get over how many pastors—several who I thought were good friends—avoided me. Some wouldn't even speak to me. And I know it was because they were upset about my appointment."

Instead of celebrating his success with him and wishing him the best in his new appointment, envy had poisoned their spirits and caused them to pull away from their colleague and friend.

Of course, envy and jealousy can result in much more than our simply pulling away from other persons. They can cause us to actively turn against them until we find ourselves gossiping about them, backbiting, slandering their reputations, using our power and influence to hinder their progress. And when we hear they're having problems or difficulties, we inwardly take delight.

But envy and jealousy not only turn us away from others; they also turn us against ourselves. Envy causes us to think, "There's something about that pastor, something about his church, something he or she is able to do that I wish I had." As a result, instead of concentrating on the things we do have and the gifts God has given us, we focus on our deficiencies. Then we feel inferior and angry at ourselves for not being like someone else. Feelings of inferiority lead to despondency which, in turn, stifles our abilities.

Sometimes to protect ourselves from such feelings, we tear other pastors down. If we can keep them on our own level, then we will feel all right about ourselves. Listen to a group of pastors at a minister's conference discussing a sermon they have just heard by someone renowned for preaching, and you'll hear comments like, "I was expecting more." "That wasn't anything to write home about," and "If we had a staff and could devote more time to preaching, we could preach like that too."

Such comments usually reveal more about us than about the guest preacher. If we can keep others on our level, we don't have to face our incompetencies or deal with our anger for not being all we'd like to be.

Out of desperation to get ahead, our envy and jealousy may even cause us to compromise our moral and spiritual integrity. Then we resort to methods contrary to the Gospel to make the church grow. Or we make sure we are noticed by the right people—those who wield power and influence in the denomination—to insure our call or apppointment to a larger church.

Envy and jealousy also turn us away from God. When we want what others have or wish we were someone else, we reject what God has ordained. We call unclean what God has called clean. We "play God" by trying to determine what others should have and what we should have. We rebel against God's will and assert our own.

The award-winning film *Amadeus,* based on Peter Shaffer's play, is a powerful study of the deadly effects of envy on all our relationships—with others, God, and ourselves. The story revolves around two characters, Antonio Salieri, the court composer for the eighteenth-century Austrian Emperor Joseph, and his rival, Wolfgang Amadeus Mozart, whom many consider the greatest musical genius of all time. Although some have questioned certain historical details of the film, the story makes a profound statement about jealousy.

When the film begins, thirty-two years have passed since Mozart's untimely death. Salieri, now an old man in an asylum, has recently tried to commit suicide. A priest comes to visit him and encourages him to make confession. So he tells the priest the story of his jealousy of Mozart and how it has destroyed him.

As a boy Salieri wanted to develop his musical talents, but his father wouldn't hear of it. He was determined his son would follow in his footsteps by pursuing a career in commerce. One day during a worship service, Salieri bargained with God. "Lord, make me a great composer," he prayed. "Let me celebrate Your glory though music, and be celebrated myself. Make me famous throughout the world, dear God. Make me immortal. After I die let people speak my name forever with love for what I wrote. In return I will give You my chastity, my industry, my deepest humility, every hour of my life."

Not long afterward, Salieri's father choked on something he was eating and died. There was no doubt in Salieri's mind that God had answered his prayer. He was now able to develop his musical talents, and eventually he became the court composer for Emperor Joseph, who was known as the musical king. Salieri was well liked by everybody at the court and he liked himself.

At the time Mozart was employed by the archbishop of Salzburg. Salieri admired the younger man's musical genius, and so he traveled to the archbishop's palace to meet Mozart and to hear the first performance of one of his symphonies. He wondered as he looked around at those gathered in the palace, "Is talent like that written on the face? Which one could he be?"

Salieri went into a large room where the food was being

served. He was alone in the room when a young woman ran in and hid underneath one of the tables. Seconds later a man who was chasing her rushed in. He soon found her under the table and the two of them frolicked and kissed on the floor. The young man was in his twenties, but he appeared to Salieri to be a vulgar, arrested adolescent.

Later Salieri got the shock of his life. That giggling, obscene creature who had been crawling on the floor was conducting the orchestra. *He was Mozart!* But his music. As Salieri described it to the priest, "This was music like I had never heard, filled with such longing. It seemed to be the music of God. Yet why would God choose such an obscene child to be His instrument?"

Because of Mozart's growing reputation, Emperor Joseph invited him to his court. He wanted to commission him to write an opera. Salieri composed a little "march of welcome" for the occasion. But when Mozart heard it, he scoffed. Then he sat down and reworked it in front of Salieri, the Emperor, and the other court musicians. Salieri was utterly humiliated.

"All I ever wanted was to sing to God," he told the priest. "He gave me that longing and then made me mute! If He didn't want me to praise Him with music, why implant the desire like lust in my body and then deny me the talent?"

Later Mozart humiliated Salieri even more by stealing away his attractive pupil Katherina and sleeping with her. In commenting on that, Salieri said, "I was in love with the girl—at least in lust. But I never touched her! ... It was incomprehensible. What was God up to? My heart was filling up with such hatred for that young man. For the first time in my life I began to have violent thoughts."

Mozart soon married his girlfriend, Constanze, and they decided to live in Vienna. One day Constanze came to Salieri with a request for help. Her husband was terrible at managing money—he spent much more than he earned. She had brought the scores of some compositions with her, and she wanted Salieri to examine them and then help her sell them. "They're all originals," she said. "He doesn't make copies."

When Salieri looked at them he was astonished. "It was beyond belief," he explained to the priest. "These were first and only drafts of music, but they showed no corrections of any kind—not one. He had simply written down music he had already finished in his head—page after page of it, as if he were just taking dictation. And music finished as no music is ever finished. It was clear to me—that sound I had heard in the archbishop's palace had been no accident. Here again was the very voice of God."

But seeing Mozart's scores was the last straw for Salieri. He would no longer serve a God who worked like this. After Constanze left, he removed the crucifix hanging on the wall and threw it into the fire. "From now on we are enemies, You and I," he said to God. "Because You choose for Your instrument a boastful, lustful, infantile boy and give me for reward only the ability to recognize the incarnation. Because You are unjust, unfair, unkind, I will block You. I swear it. I will hinder and harm Your creature on earth. As far as I am able, I will ruin Your incarnation."

From that point on in the film, although he pretended to be his friend, Salieri plotted and schemed to destroy Mozart. Finally, by forcing Mozart to work when he was already exhausted, Salieri brought about his untimely death.

Now thirty-two years later, although Salieri was tormented by what he did, he was still angry at God. He vented his fury on the priest, "Your merciful God . . . He destroyed His own beloved. He killed Mozart and kept me alive to torture — thirty-two years of torture, slowly watching myself become extinct. My music grew fainter, all the time fainter, while his grew louder and louder."

In the film's final scene, Salieri turned his anger on himself, "I will speak for you, Father. I speak for all the mediocrities in the world. I am their champion. I am their patron saint. Mediocrities, I absolve you."

Envy and jealousy. What deadly poison they are! They isolate us from others, divide us from our true selves, and turn us against God. No wonder the Christian tradition has numbered envy among the Seven Deadly Sins. Once unleashed in a person's heart, what a destructive green-eyed monster it can be. "Anger is cruel and fury overwhelming, but who can stand before jealousy?" (Proverbs 27:4)

The Roots of Envy and Jealousy
Why is envy such a temptation for ministers? Because I myself have struggled intensely with such feelings, I have often

reflected on that question. By describing my own experience, I believe I can shed light on it.

I happen to be the son of a very successful father who is well known in many Christian circles. He is an outstanding preacher, a gifted counselor, and a best-selling author. One of his books, *Healing for Damaged Emotions,* has sold nearly a million copies and has been translated into seventeen different languages.

Like many boys I grew up assuming that if I was going to be somebody, I had to measure up to the standard Dad had set. I had to be successful in my ministry like he was; other people had to notice me and my accomplishments as they noticed his.

Earlier I described how my struggle with the issue of success in ministry came to a head in one of my first pastorates. But the issue of having to be popular didn't really come into focus until several years later when I became a professor at Asbury Theological Seminary.

There are some wonderfully gifted people on our seminary faculty. As I began to work among them, I found myself feeling like a little frog in a big pond, like a sapling growing up in the shadow of big trees.

Soon I was struggling with feelings of jealousy toward certain members of the faculty. I found myself competing with them—I had to be a more popular professor, a more productive writer, and a more sought-after speaker than they were. How ironic that I was in a support group with several of the persons I was competing with! Often when we would get together and they would describe all the exciting things they were doing, instead of being able to rejoice with them, I would go away depressed. In comparison I felt small and insignificant.

It was then that God began to show me how growing up in the shadow of my father had affected me. I had determined that to be worthwhile as a person, I had to be as prominent and famous as he was. Now because I wasn't measuring up to those standards, I was frustrated and discouraged.

I also came to realize that what I was doing was absolutely antithetical to everything I believed about what gives a Christian self-worth. I was seeking to establish my self-worth on the basis of my accomplishments and the recognition of those accomplishments by others. Yet I knew that according to the Gospel, our self-worth is a gift from God. It is not based on our ability to preach, the size of our church, or the number of books we write. It is based simply on the fact that in Christ, God declares we are His children. And that is not merely what we are called, that is what we are! (See John 1:12; 1 John 3:1.) We are beloved by God (Romans 1:7). Why? Simply because He says so! Our self-worth then is not a reward to be achieved; it's a gift to be received.

By insisting on establishing my self-worth on the basis of accomplishments and acclaim, I was rejecting God's gift of self-worth. Worse than that, I was playing God. For I was defining what makes one worthwhile, and then living by that definition, instead of accepting God's definition and living by it. To reject God's way and insist on our own is sin. I finally acknowledged it as such and repented of it.

Now I was aware of my problem. I knew what the roots of my envy and jealousy were. I realized they were bound up with my relationship with my father. I also knew that what I was doing was contrary to what I believed as a Christian.

But although I had gained psychological and spiritual awareness of the problem, I still wasn't free. It still continued to defeat me, and so I was doubly frustrated. Like the Apostle Paul in Romans 7, I knew what was wrong, but I found myself unable to do much about it. Finally as my desperation intensified, I began to cry out to God, "Lord, I don't like what I'm doing. It's making me miserable. It's also an abomination in Your sight. You've shown me why I'm doing it, but I still keep doing it. I give up, Lord. Heal me and set me free."

Several months later in a chapel service at the seminary, God answered my prayer. A guest district superintendent was delivering the sermon. I hardly remember anything he said, but I do remember the Holy Spirit was powerfully present in our midst. During the sermon something happened. It wasn't dramatic or emotional, but in those moments God came and touched me. He sent forth His Word and healed me (Psalm 107:20). The brokenness within me was mended. He set me free not to have to be famous like my father. He set me free to be myself. And what freedom that is! For when you're sure of who you are in Christ, what other people are doing just doesn't matter anymore.

Of course, I would not want to leave the impression that since then I have never struggled with envy and jealousy. I still do sometimes, but it's no longer an uphill struggle. The normal outcome now is victory, not defeat. I am able to overcome rather than be overcome, and I praise God for that. I am also thankful that I can talk about issues like these with my father. He has been a tremendous source of support and encouragement to me.

My purpose in describing my experience is to show that envy and jealousy are generally rooted in a perverted desire for self-worth. If we base our self-worth on how well we perform, when others do as well or better than we, they threaten the way feel about ourselves. Self-worth then becomes something we have to earn.

And not only do we have to earn it, but we also have to *compete* for it. For us to win, someone else has to lose. Our worth comes from our superiority to our competitior. We are worthwhile only to the extent that we are better—more talented, more accomplished, more acclaimed, more spiritual than someone else.[3]

No wonder we become angry at those who outdo us and then look for ways to bring them down to our level. Our self-worth depends upon it! We have to be one up in order to feel good about ourselves. But there is a better way!

The Cure for Envy and Jealousy

What is the antidote for the poison of envy and jealousy? We can begin to answer that question by returning to Peter's conversation with Jesus. When he heard Jesus' prediction concerning his death followed by the call to follow, Peter "turned and saw the disciple whom Jesus loved was following them" (John 21:20).

That was where he made a big mistake. He took his eyes off of Christ. And it is clear that Peter didn't do this because John was distracting him or trying to get his attention. The text literally says, "Turning around, Peter saw the disciple whom Jesus loved."

Peter *chose* to turn and look at John. John was not in his natural line of vision—Jesus was. John was following behind them. Peter made a deliberate decision to turn his eyes away from Jesus and direct them toward John. Giving John his attention was his mistake.

Whatever gets your attention gets you. It was because Peter chose to give his attention to John, instead of keeping it fixed on Jesus, that he blurted out his complaint, "Lord, what about him?"

Jesus' stern rebuke was an attempt to get Peter's focus back on Him. The rebuke consists of two parts. First, a question, "What is that to you? Why are you concerned about John, Peter? His future—what business is it of yours?" Second, a command, "You must follow Me. Look at Me, Peter. Get your eyes back on Me."

The first part of the rebuke obviously leads to the second. How can Peter focus his attention on Jesus again until he first gets his eyes off John? The question, "What is that to you?" is Jesus' way of saying, "Stop looking at John."

But the second part of the rebuke also leads to the first. "If you follow Me," Jesus is saying to Peter, "if you have your gaze fixed upon Me, if you understand who you are in relationship to Me, then you'll be able to say about John or anybody else, "What is that to me? Do to them, Lord, whatever pleases You. Because I'm secure in Your love, it really doesn't matter."

1. The first antidote to envy, then, is to keep our eyes fixed on Christ and His great love for us. The world, the flesh, and the devil are constantly saying to us, "You are what you produce," and "You are what others say you are." But God says to us, "You are My beloved children."

Those words define our identity. We are God's beloved sons and daughters. When we are certain of who we are in Christ, then we are free to simply be what we were created to be—nothing more or nothing less. What other people accomplish and the acclaim they receive really don't matter. It is enough to know we are loved by God and that He takes pleasure in us.

Yet how easy it is for us to forget this. Like the elder brother in the Parable of the Prodigal Son, we ministers need to constantly be reminded of the Father's love. Although he lives in his father's house and works with him, the elder brother doesn't understand who he is. As a result, when his younger brother returns home, he gets angry at his father's lavish demonstration of love. He sulks and refuses to join in the celebration.

His father is grieved and pleads with him to come to the

feast. But he grumbles, "I've been slaving for you all these years yet you never had a feast like this for me." He is jealous of his younger brother because he interprets what his father has done as preference for him. So his father has to remind him of what he has so obviously forgotten, "My son, you are always with me, and everything I have is yours" (Luke 15:31).

We too need to hear those words. Our Heavenly Father is saying them to each of us, "You are always with Me. All that I have is yours." What's more, we must be intentional about putting ourselves in the divinely ordained places, through prayer, the reading of Scripture, involvement in worship and the Lord's Supper, and participation in Christian community where we clearly hear the Father saying them to us. Only when our identity is rooted and nourished in His unconditional love will our hearts be immune to the infection of envy and jealousy.

2. Acts of kindness and generosity are a second antidote to these poisons of the spirit. "Love is kind," says Paul. "It does not envy" (1 Corinthians 13:4). Kindness and absence of envy go together. The Christian tradition has maintained that the contrary virtue for this deadly sin is brotherly love, and the contrary beatitude is, "Blessed are the merciful." If we go out of our way to be kind and merciful to those we envy, there will be little soil in our hearts in which envy can grow.

We can begin by praying for the persons we envy. We can intercede for them, hold them up before God, pray God's blessing upon them, that He might prosper them and meet their needs according to His riches in Christ Jesus. We can pray for their families and for their ministries.

When we do this we put ourselves on God's side. We begin to see and care for people as God does. They are not our competitors, but our co-laborers in Christ's ministry. Our prayers will not only bless *them;* they will also bless *us.* The envy and jealousy will be replaced by love and compassion.

Along with our prayers, we should engage in specific acts of generosity and kindness toward those we envy. Brian Whitlow tells of a monk who disliked one of the brothers in the monastery. The man came from a country which was traditionally an enemy of his native land. Living together in close contact, many of the things the other brother did irritated him. He disliked how he sang and ate and did his work.

Recognizing the ill will in his heart, the monk set out to fight against it with brotherly love. He advanced the other man's interests whenever he could. He was especially courteous and kind to him. When he became sick, the monk nursed him back to health.

One day when the two men had grown old, the second monk drew the other aside and said, "Brother, I've often wondered, what is it about me that you've liked so much?"[4]

There is a wonderful old word for a generous gift, "largesse," that comes from the word *large.* What spacious air it breathes! There is no room for envy and jealousy in hearts which give such gifts.

Peter must have heeded Jesus' rebuke, for there is no further indication in the New Testament of any envy or ill feeling toward John. The picture in the Book of Acts is just the opposite, Peter and John laboring for Christ side by side, together healing a crippled beggar, standing courageously before the Sanhedrin, exercising apostolic oversight (Acts 3–4).

What about your heart? Have you let the infection of envy and jealousy toward other ministers spread in it? If so, then like Peter, hear Jesus' word and let it heal your disease, "What is that to you? You must follow Me."

Chapter Six
Receive the Holy Spirit

Unless the Holy Spirit fills, the human spirit fails.

E. Stanley Jones

Through His conversation with Peter, Jesus has been reminding us about basic essentials of ministry. He has also been renewing our passion for ministry. We have heard His question, "Do you love Me?" His command, "Feed My sheep," His prediction, "You will go where you do not want to go," His call, "Follow Me," and His rebuke, "What is that to you? You must follow Me."

But there is one other word of Jesus we need to hear. This word of the risen Christ is not found in His conversation with Peter. It was spoken earlier to the disciples when He first appeared to them following His resurrection.

It was Easter Sunday evening. The disciples were gathered together with the doors locked. Peter and John had confirmed the reports of the women that the tomb was empty and Jesus' body was gone. Mary Magdalene had even claimed He was alive and that she had seen Him. The disciples were confused and perplexed, but most of all afraid. The Jewish authorities would assume they had stolen the body and would be coming to arrest them.

Then the risen Christ appeared in their midst. He spoke peace to them and showed them His hands and side. The disciples were overjoyed—their crucified Lord really was alive! Afterward Jesus spoke peace to them again and commissioned them for ministry, " 'As the Father has sent Me, I am sending you.' And with that He breathed on them, and said, 'Receive the Holy Spirit' " (John 20:21-22).

"Receive the Holy Spirit." Unless we hear this word of Jesus, we will never be able to follow through in our response to His other words to us. Martin Luther said that the Gospel is both a demand and an offer. We have heard the demand, "Love Me, feed My sheep, Go where you don't want to go, Follow Me, What is that to you—follow Me." Now we need to hear the offer, "Receive the Holy Spirit." If we fail to hear the offer, we will never be able to meet the demand. Without the offer, the demand only leads to frustration and defeat.

The Indispensable Requirement

At the very end of His ministry, Jesus began teaching His disciples about the Holy Spirit (John 14–16). It was better for Him to go away, He said, for then the Helper, the Holy Spirit, would come. "He lives with you and will be in you" (John 14:17). "He will bring glory to Me by taking from what is Mine and making it known to you" (16:14). "He will guide you into all truth. . . . He will tell you what is yet to come" (16:3)

Following His resurrection, Jesus charged the disciples not to immediately launch into ministry. Their first order of business was to tarry in Jerusalem until they were endued with power from on high (Luke 24:49). They were to wait until they received the Holy Spirit, the promise of the Father. Only then would they be able to witness and minister in His name. From the account in Acts, we know the disciples heeded Jesus' instructions. They did tarry, and on the Day of Pentecost, the Holy Spirit came in power!

From that point on, we encounter the Holy Spirit in almost every chapter of Acts. Some have therefore suggested the book ought not be titled the Acts of the Apostles but the Acts of the Holy Spirit. Undoubtedly, the Holy Spirit is the chief actor, the prime mover throughout the book. The apostles were able to do what they did because they were Spirit-controlled, Spirit-empowered, and Spirit-filled. Their actions were rooted in and flowed out of the Spirit's actions.

The Holy Spirit, then, is the indispensable Person, and being "filled with the Spirit" is the indispensable requirement for Christian ministry. That's why throughout Acts persons are described as being filled with the Spirit:

● Jesus Himself was able to carry out His ministry because He was "anointed . . . with the Holy Spirit and with power" (Acts 10:38).

● The 120 who were gathered in the Upper Room on the Day of Pentecost were "filled with the Holy Spirit" (2:4).

● Peter was "filled with the Holy Spirit" when he addressed the Sanhedrin (4:8).

● After they had prayed, the believers were "filled with the Holy Spirit and spoke the Word of God boldly" (4:31).

● Stephen was chosen because he was "full of faith and of the Holy Spirit" (6:5). Later, "full of the Holy Spirit," he courageously bore witness and died as a radiant martyr (7:55).

● Paul was "filled with the Holy Spirit" (9:17) when Ananias laid hands on him. On his first missionary journey, "filled with the Holy Spirit," he confronted Elymas the sorcerer (13:9).

● Barnabas, Paul's companion in ministry, was also "full of the Holy Spirit and faith" (11:24).

Repeatedly, then, the leaders of the church were said to be filled with the Spirit. This qualification was considered essential for the work of ministry.

What exactly does it mean to be filled with the Spirit? Sometimes the word "filled" can be misleading. A picture of a liquid being poured into a passive, empty receptacle comes to mind. The fullness of the Spirit then is associated with a peak emotional experience where one has an overwhelming awareness of the Spirit's presence.

Such experiences may occur when persons are filled with the Spirit. However, the word "filled" in the New Testament reveals a different emphasis. To fill something has to do with taking possession or control of it. For example, when Jesus healed the paralytic who had been lowered down through the roof, the people were "filled with awe" (Luke 5:26). Likewise, in his farewell discourse, Jesus said to His disciples, "Because I have said these things, you are filled with grief " (John 16:6). These emotions—fear in one case, grief in another—had taken possession and control of them to the exclusion of other emotions. Similarly, when Paul commanded believers not to get drunk with wine but to "be filled with the Spirit" (Ephesians 5:18), he was saying, "Don't be influenced or controlled by alcohol; be controlled by the Holy Spirit."

To be filled with the Spirit, then, is to be mastered and controlled by the Holy Spirit. Every part of us, heart, mind, soul, and strength, is made available to the Spirit and brought under His influence. And since the Holy Spirit is none other than the Spirit of the risen Christ, it follows that to be Spirit-filled is to be Christ-controlled.

The prerequisite for being filled with the Spirit is total surrender, absolute submission, moment-by-moment yieldedness to the Holy Spirit. If we insist on being in control, we will never know the Spirit's fullness. The Holy Spirit is gentle like a dove and will not take control of us against our will. We have to turn control of ourselves over to Him.

God was able to work so mightily through the early apostles because they had yielded control of themselves to the Holy Spirit. They were willing to do what the Spirit prompted them to do, even when it seemed strange, illogical, or uncomfortable.

For example, Philip the evangelist was in the midst of revival in Samaria. Many were coming to Christ through his preaching. But the Spirit urged him to leave the place where he was evangelizing and head south to the desert. Did it make sense? Probably not. Why go where there is nobody, when many are responding to the Gospel? But Philip obeyed, and as a result the Ethiopian official was converted, and the Gospel gained a foothold in Africa (Acts 8:4-8, 26-40).

Peter was reluctant to obey, but the Spirit was persistent. Finally He was able to push Peter out of his comfortable Jewish cocoon. Even though it was not kosher, he entered the house of Cornelius. Then the Holy Spirit came upon the Gentiles (Acts 10).

As the church in Antioch was worshiping, the Holy Spirit said, "Set apart for Me Barnabas and Saul for the work to which I have called them" (Acts 13:2). Barnabas and Saul— their two most gifted leaders—why take them? Weren't they still needed for the work in Antioch? But the church let them go.

In his missionary travels, Paul was obedient to both the restraint and the constraint of the Holy Spirit (Acts 16:6-10).

The leaders at the Council of Jerusalem had various opinions on the Gentile question, but in the end what "seemed good to the Holy Spirit and to us" prevailed (Acts 15:28).

In each case, these Christians submitted themselves to the Holy Spirit. They yielded control and obeyed the voice of the Spirit. That is what it means to be filled with the Holy Spirit.

From the Discipleship Phase to Life in the Spirit

In his fascinating book, *Maturing in the Christian Life: A Pastor's Guide,* Neil Hamilton contrasts what he terms "the discipleship phase of the Christian life" with "life in the Spirit." In their early years of ministry, he believes most pastors are in the discipleship phase. He claims that "many of us spend half our careers under the spell of the illusions of the discipleship phase."[1]

What characterizes the discipleship phase and what are its illusions? In this phase we, like the first disciples, have heard the call of Christ, stepped out of the crowd, and left everything behind to follow Him. We have moved out of nominalism to a definite active level of commitment to the person of Christ, and we are seeking to follow in His footsteps.

But there are two major illusions we suffer from during the discipleship phase—illusions which keep us from hearing the offer, "Receive the Holy Spirit." Both of these illusions surface in the Gospel account where James and John come to Jesus with a request, "Teacher, we want You to do for us whatever we ask."

When Jesus asks, "What do you want Me to do for you?" James and John quickly respond, "Let one of us sit at Your right and the other at Your left in Your glory."

Jesus replies, "You don't know what you are asking." Then He questions them, "Can you drink the cup I drink or be baptized with the baptism I am baptized with?" To which James and John confidently reply, "We can" (Mark 10:35-39).

Like James and John, in the discipleship phase we too have an illusion about our ability to follow Jesus. Hamilton suggests that their reply, "We are able," is "the motto of the discipleship phase."[2] We are still confident in ourselves, confident that out of our own ego strength we can follow Jesus and advance His kingdom.

"We can do it." With commitment, hard work, drive, and determination, we can be faithful and successful, or so we think. Peter was adamant, "Even if I have to die with You, I will never disown You" (Mark 14:31). We too overestimate ourselves. That is the first illusion of the discipleship phase.

The second is an illusion concerning the nature of Christ's kingdom. When James and John come with their request, Jesus and the disciples are on their way to Jerusalem. He has just reminded them that He is going there to be crucified, but they won't believe it. Instead James and John are thinking, "He's finally going to do it. He's going to declare war on the Romans and drive them out of the land. He'll march triumphantly into Jerusalem, claim the throne, and set up the messianic kingdom. Now is the time to put in requests for cabinet positions in the new government Jesus will establish!"

"We want You to do for us whatever we ask." That, says Hamilton, is the most commonly heard request in the discipleship phase. "Let one of us sit on Your right and the other on Your left." We have a self-serving vision of Christ's kingdom. We want to advance His kingdom in order to advance our own. We follow Christ, but we want Him to take us where *we* want to go. These are the illusions of the discipleship phase, and because many younger pastors are under their spell, their ministry is affected by them.

The pastor assumes, "I can make it happen. With all my energy and determination and hard work, with all I've learned in seminary, I can turn this church around. Spiritual renewal, numerical growth, increased involvement in mission and outreach—it will happen. Under my leadership this congregation will come alive. And when my superiors and the other churches in the denomination find out about it, they'll know I'm an effective pastor. I'll be called or appointed to a larger church. I'll advance Christ's kingdom and I'll also advance my career."

But it doesn't quite work out the way we planned. We run up against the brick wall of the typical local church! As Hamilton describes it:

> The reality is that the vast majority of persons in a typical congregation do not want themselves or their world to be transformed by the Gospel. Instead,

they want the minister to help them make life easier to manage while they and their world stay the same in every important respect. The Gospel says that we and the world orders in which we live must be changed to enjoy its blessings. The good news most people want to hear is that we can be blessed without anything changing. For most beginning clergy that is a wrenching revelation.[3]

So reality begins to sink in. The congregation's conception of the ministry is different from ours. We want to be change agents; they want us to support the status quo. And we realize they have more power to change us than we have to change them!

Unfortunately, at this crisis point many young pastors choose to shift their focus. In the place of passion for change, they put pursuit of career. Hamilton says it well:

Caught in the backwash of broken dreams of being change agents, young clergy shift toward pursuit of career as an alternative future. Advocacy of personal and social transformation fades as a major preoccupation of ministry. Career becomes the dominant eschatology for the profession. An unspoken contract gets struck. If we exert ourselves to provide what the institutional church wants at local and denominational levels, we will be rewarded with career advancement. From this point on, our ministries tend to be driven by pursuit of career rather than by passion for change.[4]

What happens to pastors who shift in this direction? They generally move forward for the next ten to fifteen years. That's how long it usually takes for career advancement to reach its peak. But ironically, says Hamilton, there comes a time for those who pursue this track when the institutional church or the denomination lets them down and they feel betrayed.

> We have contracted with the institutional church for career advancement. Then the institution fails to keep its part of the bargain. Sometime in our forties or fifties we realize we will rise no higher. There will be no larger or more challenging parishes to lead.[5]

Now the minister is at another crisis point. But thank God there is a way out! Both of these crises—that of the young pastor confronted with the congregation's resistance to change and of the middle-aged pastor feeling betrayed by the institution—hold out the possibility of transition from the discipleship phase to life and ministry in the Spirit. Through these crises we finally die to the illusions of the discipleship phase.

In the case of the disciples, it also took a crisis, the tragedy of Golgotha. No longer were they declaring, "We are able." They had all forsaken Jesus in His hour of need.

When he heard the cock crow, Peter realized what he had done and "went outside and wept bitterly" (Luke 22:62). Now he was broken and humbled. His illusory confidence in himself had been shattered.

"We had hoped that He was the One who was going to redeem Israel," the two disillusioned disciples told the mysterious stranger, as they walked along the road to Emmaus (Luke 24:21). But Jesus, the One they were counting to be the Messiah, was dead. All their selfish, nationalistic messianic expectations were gone.

How traumatic the crucifixion of Jesus was for the disciples! But how necessary. It forced them to die to their illusions. More importantly, it brought them to the place where they were finally ready to hear the risen Christ's offer, "Receive the Holy Spirit." Our experience is similar. As Hamilton expresses it:

> Selves formed in the service of these illusions must suffer a psychic death of disillusionment before new selves may be formed. . . . But the first grand dreams of discipleship die hard. There seems to be no way around some trauma in the process of the psychic death and dying that accompanies the dispelling of illusion.[6]

But out of the psychic death precipitated by crisis points in ministry comes new life and ministry in the fullness of the Spirit. Worn out, exhausted, sick and tired of being sick and tired, we are finally ready to hear Christ's offer, "Receive the Holy Spirit."

Life and Ministry in the Fullness of the Spirit
What characterizes life and ministry in the fullness of the Spirit? In reading again the familiar account of Pentecost (Acts 2:1-4), I was struck by the outward, external signs which were present when the Holy Spirit came upon the disciples. Individually and together, those signs — wind, fire, speaking in tongues — offer a beautiful summary description of life and ministry in the fullness of the Spirit.

1. It's a life and ministry of *power.* Throughout Scripture, *wind* represents the divine energy, the life force, the breath of God.

In Ezekiel's vision of the valley of dry bones, God asks the prophet, "Son of man, can these bones live?" Ezekiel can only answer, "O Sovereign Lord, You alone know" (Ezekiel 37:3). Then God declares to the bones, "I will make breath [the Hebrew *ruach* also means wind or spirit] enter you, and you will come to life" (37:5).

When the wind of the Spirit blows upon us, we too are empowered and energized. "You will receive power," promised Jesus, "when the Holy Spirit comes upon you" (Acts 1:8). As Hamilton puts it, "The limited energy of a self misguided by illusion drove the life of discipleship. Now the life . . . is driven by the unlimited energy of the Holy Spirit."[7]

The late Paul Rees used to say that to be filled with the

Holy Spirit is to have "a quiet sense of the divine adequacy." Adequacy . . . power to live the Christian life. The words of Edwin Hatch's familiar hymn say it well:

> Breathe on me, Breath of God.
> Fill me with life anew.
> That I might love what Thou dost love,
> and do what Thou wouldst do.

In contrast, picture a man in a sailboat on a large lake. It's a perfect day for sailing. There's not a cloud in the sky, and sunshine glistens on the water. A steady breeze creates gentle swells on the lake.

Everything is perfect—except that the boat's sail is down and the man in the boat is using a paddle. He's paddling as hard and as fast as he can. Sweat is pouring off his forehead. But in spite of all his effort, the sailboat is hardly moving.

That is also a picture of many pastors: expending incredible amounts of energy in ministry, worn out and exhausted, yet making very little progress.

We want to shout to them as we would to the man in the sailboat, "Hoist the sail! Put away your paddle and hoist the sail! Quit taking the burden of ministry upon yourself. Quit striving to be like Jesus in your own strength. Let the Spirit of Jesus, the Holy Spirit, empower you and reproduce the life and ministry of Jesus in you. Let the mighty rushing wind of the Spirit blow upon you and move you along."

2. It's a life and ministry of *purity*. The tongues of fire on

the Day of Pentecost represent the sanctifying, purifying work of the Holy Spirit. He comes as a refiner's fire to melt down and burn away the dross and impurities in our lives.

At the Jerusalem Council when Peter described how the Holy Spirit had come upon the Gentiles in the house of Cornelius, he stressed the purging, purifying action of the Spirit. The Holy Spirit came upon them just as He came upon us, said Peter, "for He purified their hearts by faith" (Acts 15:9). Thus God's promise given through the Prophet Ezekiel centuries before was fulfilled, "I will cleanse you from all your impurities and from all your idols. I will give you a new heart and put a new spirit in you" (Ezekiel 36:25-26).

What does it mean to be pure? That which is pure consists of one thing and one thing only. It is unmixed with any other matter. It contains nothing which does not properly belong. Gold which contains no alloy is pure gold. A pure heart, then, is a heart undivided in its loyalties. It is single and united in its desire to do God's will. Søren Kierkegaard was right, "Purity of heart is to will one thing."

However, as we walk with Christ and seek to minister for Him, we soon discover how impure our hearts really are. Like the disciples, we have a self-serving vision of the kingdom. We want to advance Christ's cause *and* our own. We resemble Bunyan's character "Mr. Facing-both-ways," in *Pilgrim's Progress.* At times we are a walking civil war. How frustrating and exhausting it is!

As Howard Thurman puts it in *The Inward Journey:*

There is nothing more exhausting for the person than the constant awareness that his life is being lived at cross-purposes. At such moments the individual seems to himself ever to be working against himself. What he longs for is the energy that comes from a concentration of his forces in a single direction, toward a single end.[8]

When the Spirit comes in His fullness, He provides that energy. As a purging, refining fire, He burns up the dross and impurity in our hearts. We are set free from the tyranny of a divided self. More and more we become single-minded in our pursuit of God. The Spirit puts within us a supreme desire not to want our own way! The will of God becomes our magnificent obsession. We become wholehearted instead of halfhearted in our love for God. We are released to minister unreservedly for Him.

3. It's a life and ministry of *productivity*. When we move into the fullness of the Holy Spirit, the gifts of the Spirit which make us productive and useful in Christian service are increasingly operative through us. The "speaking in other tongues" on the Day of Pentecost represents this.

Jewish pilgrims from all over the world who had gathered in Jerusalem for the Feast of Pentecost heard the disciples speaking in their own languages and dialects. "We hear them declaring the wonders of God in our own tongues!" (Acts 2:11) Then Peter preached and the people were so cut to the heart they didn't let him finish his sermon, but cried out, "Brothers, what shall we do?" (Acts 2:37) When Peter told them to repent and be baptized in Jesus' name, 3,000 responded.

After Pentecost the disciples were effective in their service for God. They were able to get the job done, to extend the horizons of God's kingdom, because the gifts of the Holy Spirit were manifest in them.

For when the Holy Spirit comes in fullness, not only the *character* of Jesus is reproduced in us, but the *ministry* of Jesus is evidenced as well. We are enabled to do the works of Jesus. He Himself promised this. "Anyone who has faith in Me," He said, "will do what I have been doing. He will do even greater things than these, because I am going to the Father" (John 14:12). These greater things are now possible because Jesus has ascended to the Father, and has sent the Holy Spirit who bestows His gifts upon us (Ephesians 4:8-12).

When the gifts are made manifest through us, as they were through the disciples, we too will be able to get the job done. If we have been given the gift of teaching, when it is in operation, people will learn; if the gift of mercy, they will be comforted. If it's administration, the organization will run smoothly; if healing, the sick will get well. If it's evangelism, persons will come to know Christ; if service, practical needs will be met.

When we minister in the fullness of God's Spirit, the gifts of the Holy Spirit become increasingly operative in us. There is an anointing bestowed upon us for the task at hand. Our service for God becomes powerful and effective.

A pastor friend told me of a crisis point in his ministry when he said to God, "Either You are cruel and unfair or there is a better way."

"I had come to the realization," he explained, "that it was utterly impossible in my own strength to do the things God had called me to do. It also dawned on me that God knew this all along! Yet wouldn't it be cruel and unfair of Him to call me to ministry, knowing I couldn't fulfill my calling? He would be setting me up for failure. Well, I *knew* God wasn't cruel and unfair. He wouldn't do that to me or to anybody, so there had to be another way. There must be divine enabling for ministry I wasn't availing myself of.

"It was then that I became hungry and thirsty for life and ministry in the fullness of the Spirit. And ever since I entered into that reality, my ministry has been different. It has been like D.L. Moody said following his experience of the fullness of the Spirit, 'I preached the same sermons I had preached before, but the results were dramatically different.' Now there is a power and effectiveness I've never known before. I am able to get the job done."

4. It's a life and ministry of *presence*. All three of the outward manifestations on the Day of Pentecost—wind, fire, speaking in tongues—are symbols of the manifest presence of God. Those gathered in the Upper Room knew beyond a shadow of a doubt that God was in their midst.

When the Spirit comes in fullness, we have an abiding sense of the presence of Christ which we have never known before. As Oswald Chambers puts it, "This aura of the Lord's presence surrounds the personality of everyone who is baptized with the Spirit of Christ."[9] The Spirit who in the time of discipleship "dwells with you," now with the transition to life in the Spirit "will be in you" (John 14:17). Through the fellowship of the Holy Spirit (2 Corinthians 13:14; Philippians 2:1), we experience an intimacy, a friendship with God which we have never known before.

Joachim of Fiore, a medieval theologian, stressed the reality of such a relationship with God through his doctrine of the kingdom of God.[10] Joachim maintained that in the history of salvation, the kingdom of God had taken particular forms corresponding to the unique nature of the three Persons of the Trinity. First there was the kingdom of the Father, then the kingdom of the Son, and finally the kingdom of the Spirit.

Joachim also believed that in our own personal salvation history, we experience the kingdom in a threefold way. We begin with the kingdom of the Father where we live under the law. Our relationship with God is that of servant to master. We recognize our utter dependence upon God, but we are in fear of God because we have not lived up to His demands.

When we move in our Christian experience to the kingdom of the Son, our relationship with God is radically changed. Now we are not under law but under grace. God is no longer a dreaded master but a beloved Heavenly Father. We are no longer servants but God's children. We belong to His family and can come boldly into His presence. We have confident access before Him.

But, according to Joachim, there is yet another level of relationship with God where we move into the kingdom of the Spirit. It incorporates what was in the former levels, but deepens and extends them. Now we live not only under grace, but under more abundant grace. God is our Heavenly Father, but now we are grown children. We experience a friendship with God where respect is combined with affection. There is adult conversation with God along with a level of intimacy and mutuality we never knew before.

Along with increased intimacy with God, the fullness of the Spirit also brings an increased constancy of His presence. Like Brother Lawrence we learn to "practice the presence of God" in the ordinary affairs of life. We find ourselves walking with God moment by moment. There is an increased sensitivity to the voice of the Spirit.

Of course, I don't want to paint an overly optimistic picture of life and ministry in the fullness of the Spirit. If I were to add a fifth characteristic to go along with *power, purity, productivity,* and *presence,* it would be *persecution.* As we begin to minister in the fullness of the Spirit, at times we will encounter intense opposition like we've never known before. Jesus did. So did the apostles. So will we.

In his description of the "ministry of the Spirit" in 2 Corinthians 4–6, Paul says we will be hard-pressed, perplexed, persecuted, and struck down. We will struggle with failures and infirmities. Because the treasure is contained in earthen vessels, and we are not in heaven yet, we will at times groan.

Lean Back

I pray that you have become thirsty for more of the Spirit in your ministry. Jesus' offer, "Receive the Holy Spirit," still stands. And it is for you! Concerning the Spirit, He said, "If anyone is thirsty, let him come to Me and drink" (John 7:37). And again, "If you then, though you are evil, know how to give good gifts to your children, how much more will your Father in heaven give the Holy Spirit to those who ask Him!" (Luke 11:13)

Believing that He wants to fill you with His Spirit, come to Him in your emptiness. Turn the control of your life over to Him. Die to your illusions about ministry. Give Him your all—and then take His all. By faith receive the Holy Spirit.

Author John Sherrill tells of an experience he had when he joined the church choir.[11] Not long after he joined he realized he had made a mistake. He couldn't sight-read. His range was narrow and his volume was puny. Other choir members encouraged him and gave him pointers, but it was no use. He began to look for a graceful way to quit.

Then one night during rehearsal, he happened to take a chair directly in front of a big Irishman named Bill Brogan. As his magnificent bass voice boomed forward, Sherrill noticed his own singing improved significantly. He commented about it after the rehearsal.

Bill said, "I'll show you something even better next week."

The following week Bill sat next to Sherrill. Halfway through the Advent chorale, he slipped behind him and whispered, "Lean back."

Sherrill was puzzled. "What do you mean?"

"Put your weight on me."

He still didn't understand, but he leaned back until his shoulder blade was resting on Bill's chest.

"And suddenly," Sherrill said, "I knew what singing was all about. The resonances of his deep voice swelled through my own; effortlessly, I made tones I hadn't known were in me."

Jesus is saying the same thing to you, "Lean back and put your weight on Me."

"Receive the Holy Spirit." That is His offer to you. The Holy Spirit will resonate and swell through you. You'll discover what ministry is all about!

Endnotes

Chapter 1

1. Henri Nouwen, *The Way of the Heart* (New York: Seabury Press, 1981), 31.
2. Elizabeth O'Connor, *Call to Commitment* (New York: Harper and Row Publishers, 1963), 94.
3. Oswald Chambers, *My Utmost for His Highest* (New York: Dodd, Mead and Company, 1935), 217.
4. Ibid., 277.
5. Ibid., 18.
6. Ibid., 293.
7. Ibid.
8. Harry Escott, ed., *The Cure of Souls: An Anthology of P.T. Forsyth's Practical Writings* (Grand Rapids: William B. Eerdmans Publishing Co., 1971), 108.
9. Quoted in Wesley Duewel, *Ablaze for God* (Grand Rapids: Francis Asbury Press, 1990), 312–13.
10. Thomas Kelly, *A Testament of Devotion* (New York: Harper and Brothers Publishers, 1941), 35.
11. Eugene Peterson, "Subversive Spirituality," *The Door* (Nov./Dec. 1991): 6.
12. Andrew Murray understood this as the root cause of prayerlessness. See his discussion in *The Prayer Life* (Springdale, Pennsylvania: Whitaker House, 1981), 13–42.
13. Andrew Murray, *The Ministry of Intercession* (Springdale, Pennsylvania: Whitaker House, 1982), 97.
14. *The Book of Hymns* (Nashville: Abingdon Press, 1964), 134.
15. Nouwen, *The Way of the Heart*, 27–28.
16. Ibid., 28.
17. Ibid., 30.

Chapter 2

1. Quoted in John Doberstein, *The Minister's Prayer Book* (Philadelphia: Fortress Press, n.d.), 354.
2. Philip Keller, *A Shepherd Looks at Psalm 23* (New York: Harper Paperbacks, 1970), 96–97.
3. Hank Whittemore, "When a Healer Needs Healing," *Parade* (14 April 1991): 5.
4. Ibid.

Chapter 3

1. See J.R. McDuff, *The Footsteps of St. Peter* (London: James Nisbet and Co., 1876), 611ff.
2. Henri Nouwen, "Where You Would Rather Not Go," *Princeton Seminary Bulletin* 3 (Fall 1982): 238–39.
3. Marshall Shelley, "The Problem of Battered Pastors," *Christianity Today* (17 May 1985): 34.
4. Ibid., 35–36.
5. John R.W. Stott, *The Cross of Christ* (Downers Grove, Illinois: InterVarsity Press, 1986), 322.

Chapter 4

1. James Smart, *The Rebirth of Ministry* (Philadelphia: The Westminster Press, 1960), 18.
2. Ibid., 20.
3. Ibid., 37.
4. Helmut Thielicke, *Encounter with Spurgeon* (Grand Rapids: Baker Book House, 1975), 1–2.
5. Oswald Chambers, *Devotions for a Deeper Life* (Grand Rapids: Zondervan, 1986), 169.
6. Quoted in Richard Foster, *Prayer: Finding the Heart's True Home* (San Francisco: Harper Collins Publishers, 1992), 193.
7. Amy Carmichael, *The Gold Cord* (New York: Macmillan, 1932), 31.
8. Dietrich Bonhoeffer, *Ethics* (New York: The Macmillan Company, 1965), 131–32.
9. Thomas Oden, *Pastoral Theology: Essentials for Ministry* (San Francisco: Harper and Row Publishers, 1983), 59–60.

Chapter 5

1. Fyodor Mikhailovich Dostoevsky, *The Brothers Karamazov* (Chicago: Encyclopedia Britannica, Inc., 1952), 173.
2. Brian Whitlow, *Hurdles to Heaven* (New York: Harper and Row, 1963), 50–51.
3. I am indebted to Robert C. Roberts for some of these insights. See his article, "I Win, You Lose," *Christianity Today* (23 April, 1990): 28–31.
4. Whitlow, *Hurdles to Heaven*, 55.

Chapter 6

1. Neil Q. Hamilton, *Maturing in the Christian Life: A Pastor's Guide* (Philadelphia: The Geneva Press, 1984), 67.
2. Ibid., 47.

3. Ibid., 69.
4. Ibid., 70.
5. Ibid., 71.
6. Ibid., 74.
7. Ibid., 85.
8. Quoted in Frederick J. Streets, "Clarification," *Christian Century* (3–10 February, 1993): 103.
9. Oswald Chambers, *Devotions for a Deeper Life* (Grand Rapids: Zondervan, 1986), 215.
10. See the discussion of Joachim's doctrine in Jurgen Moltmann, *The Trinity and the Kingdom* (San Francisco: Harper and Row, 1981), 203–9.
11. John Sherrill, *They Speak with Other Tongues* (New York: McGraw-Hill Book Co., 1964), vii–viii.